Fixed

global fixed-gear bike culture
Andrew Edwards and Max Leonard

Laurence King Publishing

Published in 2009 by Laurence King Publishing Ltd
361-373 City Road
London EC1V 1LR
United Kingdom
Tel: + 44 20 7841 6900
Fax: + 44 20 7841 6910
e-mail: enquiries@laurenceking.com
www.laurenceking.com

Reprinted 2010, 2011

A catalogue record for this book is available from the
British Library

ISBN: 978-1-85669-645-6

Design: Andrew Edwards
Picture Research: Andrew Edwards and Max Leonard
Senior Editor: Sophie Page
Printed in China

People who spend most of their natural lives riding iron bicycles over the rocky roads of this parish get their personalities mixed up with the personalities of their bicycle as a result of

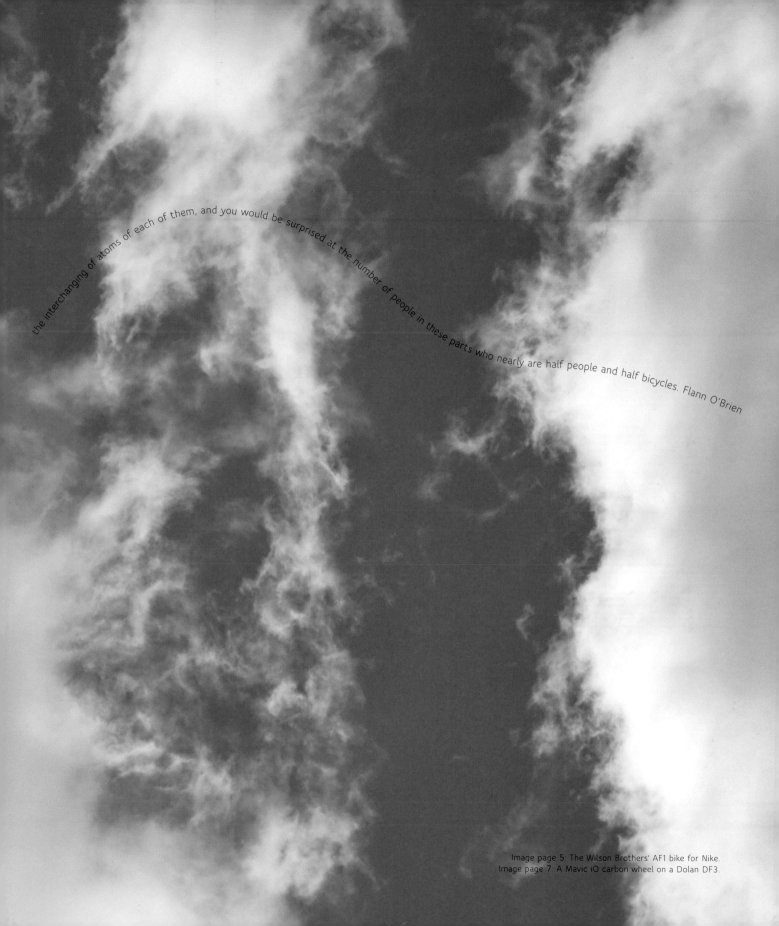

the interchanging of atoms of each of them, and you would be surprised at the number of people in these parts who nearly are half people and half bicycles. Flann O'Brien

Image page 5: The Wilson Brothers' AF1 bike for Nike.
Image page 7: A Mavic iO carbon wheel on a Dolan DF3.

Contents

Introduction

'You can always add something to the bike, but you come to the point where you can't take any more away, and that's a fixed-wheel bike.'
Graeme Obree

'Track bikes are a gateway drug to all forms of cycling.'
Mike and Gabe, Mash SF

The bicycle is often cited as humanity's most important invention, and the fixed gear is the bicycle stripped to its basics, at its most elemental, the purest expression of the diamond-framed form.

Why have they become so popular? A fixed gear is the most efficient way a person can propel him- or herself around a banked wooden oval. Fixed-wheel bikes (the British term for a fixed gear) have also long been used by British club riders looking for a shortcut to maintaining form through the dark, wet winter. Now, in cities around the world, thousands are following the example of bike messengers and are using track bikes and road conversions as a means of transport, escape and release... simply riding because a fixed gear is so fun. The bike is a blank canvas upon which riders express an individuality, or a community. Stripped down and spartan, its simplicity and purity are expressed both in the clean lines of its design and in its ride.

This book stems from our love of riding fixed in the city, through the countryside and on the track, and from our fascination with the bike as a design object. Unlike Lance's book, it is all about the bike. The diamond-framed fixed-gear bikes ridden today are fundamentally the same as those built in the nineteenth century. They are a tangible link to cycling's roots, to the early Tour de France and the brutal six-day races; our point of contact - however small - with the formidable cyclists who took on the Hour, and with the Olympic athletes and Keirin racers of today. And they are an aesthetic reference point shared with the designers and artists who have helped shape fashion and street culture. Riding fixed is an experience common to messengers, hill bombers, track stars, tricksters, street kids and commuters around the world.

There is not one fixed culture but hundreds, and this book is not a definitive history of the fixed-gear bike. Instead it is an exploration through interview, image and archive of why these bikes are special. It traces the intersections between form, function, style and culture - the knot of associations and influences at the heart of the obsession. Here are a few telling snapshots of a machine, its racing glories and its appearance on our city streets.

While researching this book, we met people pushing riding and bike design to the limits. We'd like to thank them all for sharing their love of bikes and cycling with us, even for a short while.

Andrew Edwards and Max Leonard

Opposite: In a two-mile challenge race from 1895, safeties prove their superiority over penny-farthings.

Above: The early evolution of the bicycle. Below: Drawings of H. J. Lawson's safety bicycle.

In the beginning, every bicycle had a fixed wheel. Velocipedes, or boneshakers, the earliest pedal-powered two-wheelers, had a direct drive, the pedals directly attached to the wheel axle. As people pushed their machines to go faster, the wheels got bigger; with a larger wheel, each push of the pedals resulted in more distance being covered.

Soon, the most advanced speed machines were high-wheelers (now more commonly known as penny-farthings). Yet higher speeds came at a price: high-wheelers were precarious, unstable machines, prone to bucking and sending their rider over the handlebars. Also, a rider's speed was still limited by his cadence and the length of his legs. The distance between the saddle and the bottom of the pedal stroke was usually no longer than his inside leg measurement, thus limiting wheel size, and riders struggled to maintain speeds of 20mph

(32kmh). James Moore, perhaps cycling's first superstar racer, set a distance of 14 miles, 880 yards in an hour (the first hour record) on an Ariel machine with a 49" wheel, in Wolverhampton in 1873.

1873 was also the year that H. J. Lawson of Brighton, Sussex, lodged a patent for the first chain-driven safety bicycle. Lawson's machine was nicknamed the 'Sussex Dwarf' because of its 23" wheels, but the chain and gearing allowed for a much larger development (the distance travelled in one revolution of the pedals) relative to the wheel size. In the English-speaking world, gear ratios are still measured in gear inches - the equivalent diameter of a direct-drive wheel producing the same development. A 48-tooth chainring and a 16-tooth cog (a 48/16 ratio) with a 27" wheel (including the tyre) produces the same development as a penny-farthing with an 81" wheel - far too tall for even the longest-legged man to pedal.

The bicycle chain is a remarkable invention. According to Mike Burrows, the famous bicycle designer, a well-oiled chain is up to 98.4% efficient in transferring energy from feet to rear wheel. It opened up cycling to the millions who would not straddle a high-wheeler and, by the mid-1880s, led to the bicycle's definitive basic shape being established. The freewheel wasn't invented until the late 1890s; all rear cogs were fixed. Since then there have been unimaginable advances in materials and technology, but the essence remains unchanged.

Opposite: The 1903 Tour de France.
Above: BSA path racer, probably pre-1901. Bicycle courtesy of Brooklands Museum.

In the first years of the Tour de France, competitors all raced fixed. Rudimentary derailleurs were available, but racers preferred the dependability and simplicity of a fixed wheel. According to cycling historian Les Woodland, they would run something like a 65" and a 48" gear on either side of a flip-flop hub, swapping to the easier gear to tackle hills. Henri Desgrange, the Tour's founder, grudgingly allowed freewheels in 1907, but famously railed against the derailleur: 'I applaud this test, but I still feel that variable gears are only for people over forty-five. Isn't it better to triumph by the strength of your muscles than by the artifice of a derailleur? We are getting soft. Come on fellows. Let's say that the test was a fine demonstration – for our grandparents! As for me, give me a fixed gear!'

These are the words of a man antipathetic to progress; they are tinged with sado-masochism and an idea of glory through suffering that persists in cycling culture today. Desgrange was being a bad loser: there had been a contest organized by the *Touring Club de France* that pitted a derailleur-equipped

cyclist against a fixed gear on a mountainous 240km (150-mile) course. The fixed rider was soundly beaten.

Desgrange's conception of the ideal Tour was of a race so arduous that only one competitor would finish. In 1903, the first stage of the inaugural race ran from the Paris suburbs 467km (290 miles) to Lyon. From Lyon they set off at 2:30am in order to reach Marseille, 374km (232 miles) away; the shortest stage was 274km (170 miles), from Toulouse to Bordeaux. This first Tour was won by Maurice Garin, who crossed the line having cycled 2428km (1508 miles) in 94 hours and 33 minutes, over six gigantic stages. In the 1904 Tour, Garin was stripped of his first-place finish for taking the train. Who could blame him?

For these road racers, cycling 14 hours a day for a shot at a prize worth many times the average yearly wage was preferable to subsisting by toiling in fields or down mines. This is not to say that Desgrange didn't make their lives as difficult as possible. When, in 1910, he sent the Tour over the

Pyrenean passes for the first time – on stony tracks through bear-populated forests – Octave Lapize, the eventual winner, famously shouted: 'You are all assassins!' at the officials waiting on the summit, before threatening to quit at the stage's end. Joanny Panel, competing in the 1911 race – the first that crossed the Alps – experimented with a derailleur, but incurred Desgrange's wrath and failed to finish. Only in 1937, when he was ill with cancer, did Desgrange relent and allow derailleurs in the Tour.

Early road bikes were essentially off-road machines, built with a very long wheelbase and balloon tyres to soak up bumps on the untarmacked roads. By contrast, the path racer pictured here, probably made by BSA before 1901, is at heart a track machine. The sloping top tube was fashionable and its 26" x 1¼" high-pressure tyres were typical, as racing on tubs was penalized in England at the time. Machines like this would have competed in a 100-mile (160km) 'road' race (real road racing was illegal) around a 3½-mile (5.6km) circuit at Brooklands in Surrey in 1907; the brake denotes its status as a 'road' and not a 'track' racer.

Opposite: Maurice Garin, winner of the first Tour de France in 1903, proudly displays his Tour-winning bike.

This page: Details of the BSA path racer.

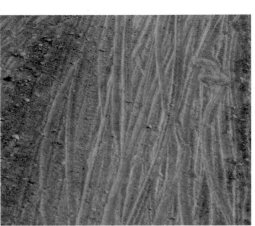

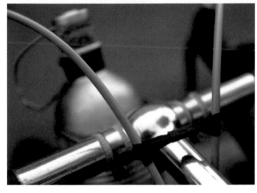

The autumn sun slants low over the Tuscan hills, the morning mists lift, and shots ring out in the distance: hunters are out stalking wild boar. Closer at hand, bicycle tyres crunch over the *strade bianchi*, the unpaved roads of white gravel that criss-cross the steep hills around Siena. L'Eroica is the foremost of the 'classic' races that challenge riders to don vintage woollen jerseys and goggles, wax their moustaches and recreate the glorious races of old.

'Never again; this is not a race for a track bike,' says Eric Von Munz, maybe the only fixed rider on the full 200km (125-mile) route. 'But each revolution of the pedal is getting me one step closer to home. I think I'm the only person here without brakes and I haven't seen many track bikes aside from the guy with the dual set-up. If you do come to L'Eroica and you want to ride it fixed, you want something like a 42/18; you want something that's just insanely weak.'

L'Eroica has now become a spring classic for the pro peloton, with riders such as Fabian Cancellara winning in around five hours, even given 65km (40 miles) of gravel. 'It's like riding on thick sand', says Eric. 'There are ruts, and it's very hard for your tyre to get any kind of a grab. Even the road bikes are having a hard time, so I'm not the only one walking up the hills, which makes me feel a little better. But I have to save my legs for the descent: whereas they can coast, I have to control the bike all the way down.' Nine hours after the pre-dawn start, the majority of the field is still going. The experience may be tame in comparison, but riding these roads on a fixed gear is the closest we'll get to the road races of a century ago.

'Oh, the other thing I'd do different?
I'd bring a fucking water bottle!' Eric Von Munz, pictured.

'20,000 FANS ARE THRILLED
Several of Riders Knocked Unconscious
in Furious Jamming That Ends Evening.'
New York Times, 1926

Opposite: Day two of the grind at Madison Square Garden, 1933.
Above: Torchy Peden of Canada (left) and Cohen of America towards the end of a six-dayer at Wembley, 1937.

On the track, six-day racing pulled in huge crowds from the early 1890s onwards, but the first six-day race took place in 1878 at the Agricultural Hall in Islington, London. Competitors raced solo for six days, grabbing sleep and sustenance when they could and only stopping on the Saturday night so as not to break the Sabbath. It was won by Billy Cann, who rode his penny-farthing in a circle almost continuously for 144 hours, covering 1060 miles (1700km).

An English entrepreneur, Tom Eck, took sixes across the Atlantic, where, in the 1890s, they were held annually at Madison Square Garden in New York. Accidents were common and, after slow nights of 'grinding', riders often connived to make their moves and sprint, or 'jam' on the Friday and Saturday evenings, to the delight of the full houses.

Spectators would offer bonuses, or 'primes' – $50, say, for the winner of a one-mile sprint - to liven up proceedings. By 1896, distances hovered around the 2000-mile (3220km) mark. That year's winner, Teddy Hale, slept only eight hours over the six days and consumed four pounds of roast chicken, four quarts of beef tea, four quarts of chicken tea, a pound of boiled rice, two bowls of custard, milk toast, jelly, tapioca and three pounds of fruit every 24 hours... as well as fish every other day.

By 1899, spectators were tiring of watching exhausted men pedal slowly around a track for so long. Riders would often fall asleep and fail to wake up even when they crashed to the boards. So the state passed laws prohibiting anyone from competing for more than 12 hours a day. This did not have

Photo by Levine Cambridge MASS.

Above: George Leander behind pacemaker Jimmy Hunter, circa 1910. In 1902, Hunter lost an eye and Leander broke his ankle when up against each other in another motor-paced event. Opposite: the 1968 Skol International six-day race at Wembley, and, bottom left, the 1977 UK National Championships.

the desired effect: canny promoters merely teamed racers into pairs and kept the 24/7 contests going, with one rider resting while the other raced. Speeds rose, the excitement returned and the crowds came back. To this day, paired races are known as Madisons in English, and *à l'americaine* in French. Nevertheless, a rider in the 1904 six resorted to affixing a horn to his bars and sounding it every 50 yards to keep himself awake. His team were under instructions to pull him in immediately if he failed to honk the horn for a lap or more.

Baseball, the Great Depression and the rise of the motorcar all conspired against the six-day race in the US. And the race's return to Europe was less than auspicious: a Toulouse six-dayer in 1906 was abandoned after three days, with the Georget brothers leading, owing to lack of interest. By 1912, however, many major northern European capitals held annual six-day races.

Ernest Hemingway loved what he described as 'the final plunge into the driving purity of speed' as the six-day sprinters launched off down the banking. 'I must write

the strange world of the six-day races,' he wrote in *A Moveable Feast*, published in 1964, recalling his time as an impoverished young man in Paris in the 1920s:

...I will get the *Vélodrome d'Hiver* with the smoky light of the afternoon and the high-banked wooden track and the whirring sound the tires made on the wood as the riders passed, the effort and the tactics as the riders climbed and plunged, each one a part of his machine; I will get the magic of the *demi-fond*, the noise of the motors with their rollers set out behind them that the *entraîneurs* rode, wearing their heavy crash helmets and leaning backward in their ponderous leather suits, to shelter the riders who followed them from the air resistance, the riders in their lighter crash helmets bent low over their handlebars their legs turning the huge gear sprockets and the small front wheels touching the roller behind the machine that gave them shelter to ride in, and the duels that were more exciting than anything, the put-puting of the motorcycles and the riders elbow to elbow and wheel to wheel up and down and around at deadly speed until one man could not hold the pace and broke away and the solid wall of air that he had been sheltered against hit him.

Above: Chris Hoy at the Laoshan Velodrome during the Beijing Olympics, 2008.
Opposite: The women's points race in the UCI Track Cycling World Cup, Beijing, January 2009.

Six-day races are still held across Europe. Craig MacLean, a British sprinter with Olympic, UCI World Championship and Commonwealth medals, frequently competed in sprinters' exhibition events at six-day races. 'For a sprinter, it feels a bit like *Groundhog Day* – you're doing more or less the same races with the same entertainment every night!' he says. 'It's a fantastic experience, some of the biggest crowds I've ever raced in front of. Berlin holds 12000 people; it's a fantastic party atmosphere, there's live music while you're riding, everyone's drinking and the track centre is crammed full of people. We race to make it look good and people respond well to it. There's not so much pressure, you can show off your skills and have fun – do track-stands and things like that which are a bit redundant these days.'

When Craig was developing as a rider in the early 1990s, there were few role models for him in British sprinting, unlike the situation for today's riders. 'When I started, you couldn't get hold of any literature on sprinting, and there was no internet. It was a bit of an underground scene, really. There was Eddie Alexander, who'd medalled at the Commonwealth Games and came fourth in the Olympic sprint in 1988 but he'd sort of retired before I started.' It is perhaps the influence of Chris Boardman and his team that has lifted British track cycling back into the spotlight. Boardman's gold medal in the 1992 Olympic pursuit on the Lotus-engineered carbon-monocoque bike inspired a new generation to cycle; a generation that formed the backbone of the medal-winning British team in 2008.

His stewardship of Team GB has also delivered some of the world's best equipment. 'Four years ago we had nothing, a blank piece of paper... where do you even start?' Boardman says. 'We assembled a group of experts and ended up producing 1786 components, helmets and different pieces of clothing that were delivered in time for the Olympics, from nothing. I can't disclose the performance advantage, but it was a ridiculously good spend.'

MacLean thinks that equipment can only go so far; but, he concedes, the psychological advantage of having the best kit is, perhaps, unbeatable. 'You have to be comfortable with what you're riding and have faith in it,' he says. 'There are times when I've had to go on to the start line knowing I'm on sub-par equipment and that's not a good position to be in – you're already on the back foot. It's so fine at the top at the moment – you're talking hundredths or thousandths of seconds – so every little thing is going to make a difference. You don't want to give yourself any disadvantage; you want to have the best available equipment.'

22

Boardman is adamant that the technology involved in the UKSI (UK Sports Institute) bike, which the British team used to such devastating effect at the Beijing Olympics, will take years to be replicated by others. 'It may inspire shapes,' he says. 'People will be studying photographs and think, "Oh, what have they done there?" and it will inspire their thinking, but it won't come out for a couple of years, you won't see it.'

In the meantime, the Dolan DF3, pictured, is perhaps the closest frame on sale commercially. The DF3 was developed in conjunction with the British sprint team, coach Ian Dyer and German star sprinter Jan van Eijden, also a coach. Framebuilder Terry Dolan has produced frames – under his own name, his brand, Cougar, and badged as other companies' frames – that have performed at the Olympics, in the Tour de France and in the Milk Race. 'We had a couple of prototypes,' he explains. 'Jan van Eijden tested the first one himself and suggested a few modifications and upgrades. Then we had feedback from the riders, Ian Dyer and Craig MacLean. The reason we called it that was we ended up putting a sticker on the top tube saying "the Dyer Flyer". So that's where we got the DF3 from... we still haven't got a name for it!'

'Carbon has always been the material of choice, given the ability to work with it and the fact that it's super-stiff and light.'
Craig MacLean

The DF3 is still a virtual prototype itself. But the UKSI bike – with which it shares looks, if not genes – will not be competitive next time round. Other countries and other manufacturers will, of course, catch up with these innovations. So what next? 'Now we've got to do it again, which is exponentially harder,' says Chris, about continuing the R&D project. 'You think you're going to get answers, naïvely, but we just came up with a load more questions; a couple of answers, but a hundred more questions.'

This mid-1970s Rih was built in Amsterdam and Italian-equipped with 3TTT and Campagnolo components (originally 151BCD, rather than the more modern 144BCD pista cranks) and Nisi rims. Rihs have won more than 350 national titles on road and track, and 63 Olympic and World Championship medals. The name, taken from a popular book of the 1920s, refers to an Arabian stallion and means 'faster than the wind'. The current owner and framebuilder joined the firm in 1948 as an apprentice. Complete bicycle supplied by Tour de Ville, London.

CARLTON

This stayer was built for racing behind
motorcycles (see image, page 18) at Reg
Harris's Fallowfield track, Manchester, but
lived out most of its life at Leicester. It
was a stock machine available for all track
users, hence the adjustable stem and saddle.
The strut on the bar keeps the saddle from
slipping. The reverse-rake fork and 24" wheel
let riders tuck in out of the wind close to
the motorcycle, reaching speeds of up to
70mph (112kmh). The gear here – 63/14
– is typical. This bike has oversized,
plain-gauge tubes for strength,
and a reinforced bottom
bracket shell to deal with
the forces passing
through it.

26

CARLTON

Bicycle courtesy of Brooklands Museum.

The Rotrax 'Vel d'Hiv' model was top of the range when it was introduced in 1949. Built in Southampton, England, the name combines 'Road' and 'Track' to reflect the machine's dual purpose. Nearly all classic British frames had the front fork drilled for a brake for this reason. This example, from 1954, has been used for time-trialling. Flint-catchers brush each tyre to prevent punctures. The brake lever, which is custom drilled to save weight, is a later addition from a BMX. When actually in competition, it would also have had a bell, as this was mandatory under the Road Time Trials Council (RTTC) rules.

'The whole fixie thing is literally reinventing the wheel.'
Buffalo Bill, former London cycle courier

Left: The tyranny of the watch. Above: Hounslow and District Wheelers on a pre-war club run.

In the UK, there is no great history of competitive stage races - road races were in fact banned by the National Cycling Union after an unfortunate incident involving a lady, a horse and a roadside ditch during a 50-mile (80km) race north of London in 1894. Subsequently, Frederick Bidlake, who had been pitched into that ditch, helped to codify time-trial riding. Gradually, a cloak-and-dagger road-racing scene grew, with riders competing at one-minute intervals, clothed in black and without numbers, to avoid the attention of the local constabulary. Courses were given codenames - G10/97, J2/9, V225 - which are still used today.

British club riders often trained through the winter on a fixed gear and TTs were also mainly ridden fixed. There is still a Medium Gear League, which limits participants to a 72" gear - a forward movement of precisely 18ft 10¼in for one complete pedal revolution. Early-season time trials were often limited, partly for the cyclist's own good. Cycling historian Les Woodland comments that the dreaded phenomenon of 'Easter Knee', much discussed in 1950s cycling journals, has disappeared now that we don't try to push a huge gear with feeble winter legs around a chilly, hilly 25. Until 1961, the National Championships 25 had never been won on gears.

Time trials were a fiercely amateur pursuit; a 1938 rule from the Road Time Trial Council stated: '...neither shall the racer have the name of his machine or maker so prominently displayed that it appears in photographs in the press.' The rationale was that advertising would compromise the amateur nature of the sport. It has been said that this is what drove framebuilders such as Hetchins, Bates and Freddie Grubb to develop distinctive frame designs, so their work was recognizable at a distance without branding. TTs were also mainly working class. Most participants had no car and rode the same bike all week, hence the mudguard eyes and brake fittings on classic British handmade frames. At the weekends, they'd carry their racing wheels to the start line on special wheel carriers, swap wheels over, remove the mudguards and compete.

Time trials remain accessible, the first competitive cycling that many British riders encounter. Chris Boardman, Graeme Obree and, more recently, Bradley Wiggins, all came from a TT background. 'All of the records I set – distance records and time – were fixed,' says Chris Boardman. 'The only one that still stands that isn't is the first stage of the Tour de France, but that was because of the nature of the course. For 25 miles,

Above, and detail, opposite: Made by Ayley's Products Ltd, Birmingham, the Alpex was an unsuccessful attempt to break into the cycle trade. This 1948/9 example is one of only three known survivors. Its distinctive frame design was a gimmick to promote recognition: the chainstays curve upwards, the opposite way from Hetchins', so as not to infringe the London firm's patent. Unfortunately this did nothing for the ride, and also meant that a large chainring and sprocket had to be used, to prevent the stays obstructing the chain. Bicycle courtesy of Brooklands Museum.

Below: The F. H. Grubb Twinlite, 1932/3.

10 miles and track records, they were all fixed-wheel.'

Clearly riding fixed did not hinder him. 'I don't think it was limiting at all. As long as you have a decent cadence range, from say 90 to 130, it isn't a limiting factor, and has many more benefits than downsides. I always used it for preparation for Tour de France prologues.'

Graeme Obree agrees: 'Most people doing time trials are thinking about how fast they can go. Whereas on a fixed wheel you're thinking about not going slow at any point, which is, in mathematical terms, a better way of winning a TT. At most TTs most riders will have gone faster than me at their fastest point of the race, but they won't go as fast time-wise. I'm concentrating on all the hard bits because there's no lazy lever.'

'Turning up on a track bike with one brake on is as simple as it can be, and riding that road as fast as you can on that single-

speed bike is the greatest simplicity of any road event. There's seemingly no tactics, no gears, nothing except to ride as fast you can in that gear.' And, psychologically, fixed can be a huge benefit. 'If you decide to race on a fixed wheel then that is a commitment,' continues Graeme. 'You've chosen the size gear you're going to ride and you're committed. Whereas with gears, you can always change down. There's no sense of commitment.'

For Boardman, 'It always appealed because it was just simple and pure. Your bike was one-third lighter and there were no decisions to be made. It comes back to the psychological in that you only had to focus on your own effort. All the other choices were stripped away.'

Hill climbs, a sub-specialism of a specialism, are another British peculiarity. Catford CC's famous event on the fringes of London and the North Downs is billed as the oldest cycle race in the world. On a hill climb, says Boardman, four-time National Hill Climb Champion, 'you tried as hard as you could to stay with the fixed wheel because of the obvious weight advantages. Again, there was the psychological aspect – all you had to consider was your own effort, and measuring that over the distance remaining. You took away a lot of risks. You couldn't slip a gear, didn't have to work out where to change. It was hugely advantageous for hill climbs, just perfect. They were beautiful events as well.'

Above: Six-time winner, Granville Sydney, in a National Hill Climb Championships. Opposite top: Ralph Wilson. Opposite: Chris Boardman in the 1988 event, on the Nick O'Pendle course. Below: Winnats Pass in the Peak District.

'There was definitely a feel to it, the responsiveness of it, like more of your energy is going towards creating forward motion. And there probably is, actually, something of a follow-through in the pedal stroke.'
Chris Boardman

Opposite: 1893, Henri Desgrange, Buffalo track, Paris. Above: Swiss cyclist Oscar Egg, a successful six-day, road and track cyclist, broke the hour record three times, setting a distance of 44.247km (27.5 miles) in 1914. His record was not broken until 1933, when Jan Van Hout attacked it in Roermond.

'The hour record is an extension of fixed-wheelism, because it's the simplest possible test of a human's ability as a cyclist,' says Graeme Obree. 'It's battering that track on your own for an hour. I mean, how much simpler can it be? You're riding the simplest bicycle in the simplest possible test: that is the ultimate possible extension of fixed-wheelism.'

Since the very beginning, cycling's greats have lined up to take on the Hour, the ultimate cycling record. Henri Desgrange, by his own admission only a mediocre cyclist, set the first official record of 35.325km (22 miles) in one hour in 1893. Lucien Petit-Breton, Coppi, Anquetil, Merckx, Moser and Indurain have all followed, adding their name to cycling's most celebrated and important palmares. Equally, some of the sports' stars try a few tests, realize the scale of the task, and quietly abandon hope of adding their name to the list. 'The hour record's biggest challenge is that there is no second place,' says Chris Boardman. 'There's a huge amount of risk involved and there's no hiding place at all. It's one of the few events that you know is going to be horrendous before you start.'

How, exactly, do you ride as fast as you can for an hour? 'The formula changes all the way through,' explains Chris. 'The commonality is: distance to go – can I sustain this effort? If the answer is "yes" then you're not going hard enough. If the answer is "no" then it's too late anyway, so you're looking for "maybe", a sensation of "maaaaybe". And that effort changes with the distance remaining. There's a constant equation going on trying to measure distance to go and effort.'

'Simplistically, it looks just like riding round in circles for an hour, and in a sense it is,' Boardman continues. 'But it's how you achieve that... Eddy Merckx was capable of going much further than me on a standard bike, but he didn't maximize his own abilities. He did a 1'08" first kilometre, at altitude, which has a huge cost implication to it. You don't get to stop and recover and then carry on. You carry that damage all the way through.'

For his attempt, at altitude in Mexico City in 1972, Merckx (opposite) rode a specially designed Colnago frame that pushed technology to its limits. 'We were the first to use some of these high-quality materials,' says Ernesto Colnago, looking back at the record. 'We made a 70g tubular tyre, spokes and handlebars out of titanium, and a frame 0.4mm thick with 0.6mm fork tubes.' Colnago worried that the bike would be ripped apart as 'the Cannibal' applied the force

to accelerate from a dead start, but, with a 52/14 gear and at 104.6rpm, Eddy pedalled 49.431km in the allotted time, before collapsing on to a stretcher.

To an outsider, it may seem that any challenger does so in the oppressive shadow of these greats; not so for Boardman. 'For me that contemplation happens after the fact,' he says. 'During, the whole point is that it's you against you. There is nobody else involved, there is nobody else responsible; there is nobody else who can help you and nobody else who can cause you to fail.' Obree, meanwhile, says: 'It gets to the point where you don't really think about anything...' He pauses for a time before continuing. 'It's almost like a dance. There are only two parts to the hour record really. You start, you see the black line and you sink into a rhythm. It's a hypnotic rhythm, almost like an African tribal dance, and the closer you get to the precipice, the more you have to hold on to that rhythm, just that rhythm, without losing control.'

Merckx's reputation and the physical pain he endured guaranteed that his record stood for 12 years, by which time it was understood that aerodynamics, and not lightness alone, was the crucial factor in flat time-trialling. In 1984, Francesco Moser twice broke the 50km (31 miles) barrier on an aero bike with full-disc wheels (the rear, 1m in diameter), initiating an arms race in which bike technology pushed the

Left to right: Eddy Merckx's back-up bike, held in the Colnago museum. The drilled chain saved 95g, the Cinelli handlebar was drilled 48 times, while hollow hub axles, a titanium stem and removed hub-bearing seals saved valuable grams and gained metres over the hour.

'How I ache, I can hardly move. It was the longest hour of my career. It was terrible; you have no idea what kind of intense effort it is until you have done it. The record demands total effort, permanent and intense. I will never try it again.' Eddy Merckx

Boardman riding in the 'Superman' position to break the record for the third time.
He described it as 'the best physical performance of my entire life, just great all round'.

record to previously unimaginable heights. Moser's feat, however, was a prologue to one of the Hour's most exciting battles, when Graeme Obree and Chris Boardman, two riders with contrasting styles, broke the record twice in less than a week. Boardman, who won an Olympic pursuit gold on Mike Burrows' famous Lotus bike, was the establishment's favourite. He brought all of his team's science and technology to bear on his hour record attempt. Obree was the lone outsider, who trained on a diet of marmalade sandwiches and built a bike out of spare parts, some of which were salvaged from a washing machine.

Actually, Obree's ride, nicknamed 'Old Faithful', was aerodynamically sound. The washing-machine bearings also helped, allowing a narrower bottom bracket for a preferential pedalling position. Graeme beat Moser's record of eight years' standing less than 24 hours after a first, failed attempt – a triumph of determination over physiological damage and fatigue. Boardman had long planned an attempt at Bordeaux Velodrome only six days later. On a beautiful carbon Corima

supplied by his *Crédit Agricole* team, he added 674m, reaching 52.270km. Graeme took the record back in Bordeaux the following year. Then, emboldened – and perhaps affronted that a relative unknown held cycling's biggest accolade – Miguel Indurain and Tony Rominger broke the hour record in quick succession.

In 1996, the Hour reached an impasse. Chris Boardman used the controversial, Obree-inspired 'Superman' position to ride 56.375km (35 miles). The UCI, deciding they had had enough of such acrobatics, banned the stance. The consensus was that in so doing the governing body had made Chris's second Hour unobtainable. No rider dared take it on... until, at the turn of the millennium, Boardman had an idea. 'People might be surprised to learn I'm one of the people who wish they just had a standard bike, and it was athlete against athlete,' he explains. 'I was always associated with technology because I was going to ride to the rules, but it wouldn't be my personal preference. Once I got to the end, we thought, "How can we finish this career in the right way?"'

Obree breaks the record for the
first time in Hamar, Norway,
riding Old Faithful. Less than
24 hours earlier he had failed,
riding a Mike Burrows-engineered
replica of his bike.

'The Hour is a thing of beauty. It's control and rhythm, technique, almost graceful, yet brutal. All of those. Precision, grace, beauty, brutality, at once.' Graeme Obree

With his trainer, Peter Keen, Boardman devised an Hour challenge on a traditional bike. 'We thought, "What a great way to finish!" After coming to notoriety linked with Lotus bikes and pointy helmets, and being involved with moving the sport to a different place technologically, to actually finish – the last thing you ever do – athlete against athlete, 30 years in the past, 30 years in the future.'

They set some simple rules and designed a traditional round-tubed, spoked-wheeled bike. A 60cm top tube (compared with a 53cm seat tube) and 14cm stem stretched Chris into an aerodynamic position; otherwise, the bike was superficially very similar to Merckx's. Initially, the project was to mark Chris's retirement, and was not UCI-endorsed. Soon, however, the officials warmed to it and created a new 'Athlete's Hour', scratching every performance since Merckx out of the record books. They also imposed rules, including making a modern helmet mandatory. 'That was 500 metres, wearing a safety helmet over a "bunch of bananas",' says Chris, of the drag this created. 'That took away all my safety margin, which was quite scary. It cost a kilometre until we filled in all the holes.' On 27 October, 2000, Chris Boardman rode his steel-framed bike 8m further than Merckx had 28 years earlier. 'The third time, I was really hoping for the sensations of the second one, but it was a horrendous grovel for an hour, for reasons I still don't fully understand,' he says. 'I would have loved to have just stopped, but it was the last thing I was going to do and that unfortunately wasn't an option.'

'I think this is one of the most beautiful records, now, on a standard bike, round tubing, steel,' says Graeme. For him, the record transcends its basic temporal, physical and mechanical conditions. 'It's a human being, alone, pushing themselves to the edge of their own personal precipice, and that is the point of the maximum human potential,' says Graeme, 'You have to go to the precipice, otherwise you won't know what your potential is. How close can you get without actually falling over the edge? Otherwise you'll walk away thinking, "I could have done more." That's the biggest single fear that I have going into an Hour record. Not even failing to break it. It's that.'

At the time of writing, Obree, born in 1965, was planning to ride a self-built lugged steel bicycle to attack the world hour record in late 2009. The bike is as long as regulations allow, with narrow bars and relaxed geometry. The long wheelbase makes it stable, yet the pushed-back saddle improves weight distribution. 'It means that the bike responds quicker and it likes to hold a straight line,' explains Graeme. 'If you can barely see the black line for exhaustion, you want a bike that'll see you home, like Tonto.'

Most noticeable, though, is the huge – 67/13 – gear, which represents a radical departure from traditional thinking. The gear encourages a rocking pedalling style, which Graeme says takes advantage of his increased strength. It also takes the strain off the arms. 'The limiting force in the modern – old-style – hour record is how long it takes your arms to go completely numb... when will my arms give up and I have to sit up into the airstream? The bigger gear means there's less weight in your arms, because you're leaning on the gear.'

'I love it when people say it's not possible, because that's what people said the first time round. Francesco Moser came out at forty-two or forty-three, and almost broke it. The stopwatch doesn't care what age you are. Physically I feel as strong as ever, and aerobically, too.'

'The reason I want to do this record is because in a lot of circles I'm seen as the guy who got super-aero and went fast, but is fundamentally an average athlete. It wasn't the case. I was aero, but not that aero, not compared to a good tri bar set-up,' he continues. 'Riding the Athlete's Hour is a good way to prove your physicality. There is a small amount of ingenuity in it, but basically now it's a point of physicality.'

Obree also believes this new track iron is his best yet: 'I can tell you that Old Faithful was all wrong. I now see Old Faithful and think, "How could I have thought that was a good idea?" That narrow bracket was a bad idea, that whole design was a bad idea. My fundamental lack of belief in my ability as an athlete led me to believe that was an advantage.'

There is an additional motivation. The current record holder, Ondrej Sosenka, a Czech who rode 49.700km (30.88 miles) in 2005, tested positive for the banned substance methamphetamine in 2008. He rode a (round-tubed) carbon bike with a 3.2kg rear wheel that supposedly created a flywheel effect. The suspicion is that this was not the only help he was receiving. 'An hour record that's not getting attacked is one that's getting forgotten about, especially in the current situation where the holder has been done for drugs,' says Graeme. 'There has to be, as George Bush would say, a regime change. At the moment I seem to be the person on the cards to do it. Balding or not, that is my quest, and I think there is a dire need for that to happen.'

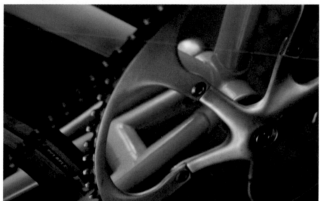

Above left: Graeme designed and built the bike that bears his signature (above). Below: The bike has no brake bridge and horizontally aligned chainstays that increase side-to-side strength. The wheels from this bike were used by Darren Kenny to set the para-cycling Athlete's Hour record in 2009 at a distance of 40.516km (25.175 miles).

In 1948, as part of its national reconstruction, the Japanese government added Keirin to the list of 'officially managed races'. Although the Japanese love to gamble, there are strict laws prohibiting betting on most sports except horse racing. However, in the postwar austerity, few people could afford to keep horses, depriving the national coffers of tax revenues and good causes of their share of the pot. So, in Kokura City in November 1948, the first Keirin (which translates as 'racing wheels') meeting was held, under the aegis of the *Nihon Jitensha Shinkokai* (NJS, now known as the Japanese Keirin Association, or JKA).

Over time, Keirin evolved into its modern form: nine competitors in a 2000m race, paced behind another rider until, with one and a half laps to go, they are released to sprint to the finish at up to 70kmh (43.5mph). 'Keirin is like a living thing,' says Koichi Nakano, the most successful Keirin rider ever. 'It has kept changing over 60 years, so the way we used to race is different from how it is now.' At the start, women's Keirin also flourished, but was discontinued in 1967; it was, say the officials, simply not as fast or exciting as the men's races – and therefore less profitable.

Street riders the world over are fascinated by Keirin, but in Japan it has long had a social stigma because of its roots in gambling and persistent rumours of corruption. Soon after it was founded, there were a number of race-fixing scandals. Punters rioted at an Osaka meeting in 1949 after a hot favourite started slowly and placed poorly. Just a week later there was mayhem when a bell-ringer in Kobe lost count of the number of laps to go. Organizers turned to local mobs to police the races, but this only led to in-fighting among rival gangs. In the 1950s, race-fixing penalties were put in place to clean up the sport's image.

Nowadays, the 47 tracks (including three covered velodromes) are patronized mainly by men, who crowd the TV screens to keep abreast of races at other tracks, treading on the losing tickets that litter the floor. It is more like a greyhound track than an athletic event. The riders wear numbered, brightly coloured jerseys over body armour, and resemble jockeys rather than Western track stars. 'When I first saw a Keirin race at Keiokaku, Tokyo, in 2001, I couldn't believe how intense it was - not comparable, of course, to the Tour going up Alpe d'Huez, but intense in such a different way,' says Mortimer Steinke, owner of the Keirin Cycle Culture Café in Berlin. 'It's brutal how they cut each other off, shove each other around. It reminds me a lot of messengering, ditching cars while riding in traffic, trying to go for that hole between the other riders.' It is partly thanks to Nakano that Keirin's domestic reputation has improved. He was the first Keirin rider to make it on the international stage, winning an unmatched ten consecutive world titles between 1977 and 1986. Keirin became an official UCI World Championship event in 1980, and its Olympic debut in 2000 in Sydney has raised it further in the eyes of many Japanese.

Previous page: A rider breaks to victory riding a Katakura Silk bike.

Opposite above: A Keirin race in view of Mount Fuji.

Opposite below: A race winner takes a victory lap.

Above: Unidentified female and male Keirin race winners.

Left: A 'cat and mouse' finish.

Above and opposite: A Keirin race in the 1960s.
Right: Koichi Nakano riding his trademark red Nagasawa.

Nevertheless, Keirin stars, who can earn millions of dollars a year, are not perceived as pure athletes. 'In Japan, Keirin is a profession,' says Nakano. 'At high school I did athletics, was a short-distance runner and then became a cyclist as a profession. The fact that both my parents were professional Keirin cyclists was a big factor.' Nakano's father, Mitsuhito, raced into his fifties; the oldest-ever Keirin rider retired at sixty, but it's a hard life. There is no off-season, and riders must race a certain number of times a month to keep their licence. For each win or place they gain points. Every six months a cut is taken: the top 50 riders go up a division, the bottom 50 go down. Of the 3900 professionals, the 860 S-class racers are the elite, the A-class racers are second-best. S class comprises two divisions; A class, three. Older riders rely on their skill and tactical expertise to beat competitors half their age and halt their slide into obscurity. Eventually, the lowest-placed A-class riders lose their licence and are replaced by recruits fresh out of Keirin school.

All professional riders must attend the Keirin school, which sits atop a windswept hill in Shizuoka province. Surrounded by landscaped gardens and three banked oval tracks, the facility, built in 1968, is half Bond-villain's lair, half Communist military installation. It is spotlessly clean; the boys (75 at a time, staying for six months) do two hours of chores between 6:30am, official wake-up time, and breakfast at 9am. Many are up earlier, rising at 4am to ride the winding country roads, searching for that edge on their classmates.

Formerly there was an age limit on admissions but, as applications have decreased, this has been lifted. As long as you pass the tests, and have no Yakuza ancestry (JKA is ever-fearful of corruption), you're in. Some are high-school track and field athletes, some are from crafts and professions, and one student in the 2008 class went to the same prestigious school as the Japanese emperor's children – another sign that attitudes are changing.

Lined up next to the banking, shaven-headed and in tracksuits, the recruits look identical. On the track they are distinguished by the colour of their helmets: black helmets denote sprint stars, red helmets, endurance riders. Those with both qualities wear white; those wearing blue are not making the grade and must try harder.

Nowadays, the training seems scientifically controlled, with ramp and VO_2 tests, but rumours speak of more primitive methods in the past – for example, two sets of rollers set up with a sheet suspended between them, the riders battling to knock the other off while staying upright themselves. Even so, the present-day regime is highly disciplined. One feared component involves sprints up a purpose-built hill, greater than 1:7 in gradient – with 15 reps being more than enough to induce vomiting. To graduate, students must ride a 1'15" kilometre, using no higher than a 49/15 gearing.

Right: Students warm up prior to sprint training in one of the school's three outdoor velodromes.

Opposite above: Each student has his own custom-made NJS-certified bike, which carries a number for easy identification.

Opposite below: Instructors drill students before getting on their bikes.

Keirin

Clockwise from top left: Students take a rest after a block of sprint training; spotlessly clean student dorms; a machine used to analyze the students' power output; students attend an etiquette lecture. Opposite above: The school bike shed houses the students' track and road bicycles. Opposite below: A noticeboard displays the day's schedule and race tactics training.

Aside from physical conditioning, visiting lecturers – including police officers and community leaders – school the trainees in moral principles. Such are the sums bet on even a minor race that each rider must be unimpeachable in their conduct and mores. Then there are tactical classes, so trainees develop a deep knowledge of the spirit and practice of Keirin. 'Sprinting is one on one, and the rules are much simpler. It's strength against strength,' says Nakano. 'In Keirin it is not just power, you have to use the power of other riders. Positioning, movement and tactics are very much part of it. So in a way there is a darker side to it. Sometimes the ones who are more cheeky can end up winning the race.'

Unlike the international Keirin race, Japanese Keirin has a large team element. In every race, riders must form alliances, grouping into 'lines' of three. Each must then declare his

tactics: *senko* riders attempt to lead their line out and win from the front; *makuri* riders sit on his wheel, protect him from attacks, then break towards the end; and *oikomi* riders take third place, protect the other two and try to sprint to win in the last 150m. These alliances are based on friendships formed at Keirin school, regional allegiances and many complicating factors. 'Personally, I didn't mind what position I was in as long as I was second in line on the last four corners,' Nakano comments. 'It was all about how I got there. It didn't matter to me who was in what position, as long as I was in that position I knew I would win nine times out of ten.' But, he adds, racing styles are changing: 'Now it is more about the lines. If the person in front doesn't move, you can't get there – whereas we would just take it. I think cyclists nowadays prefer to settle positions without too intense a competition. I think it should be tougher.'

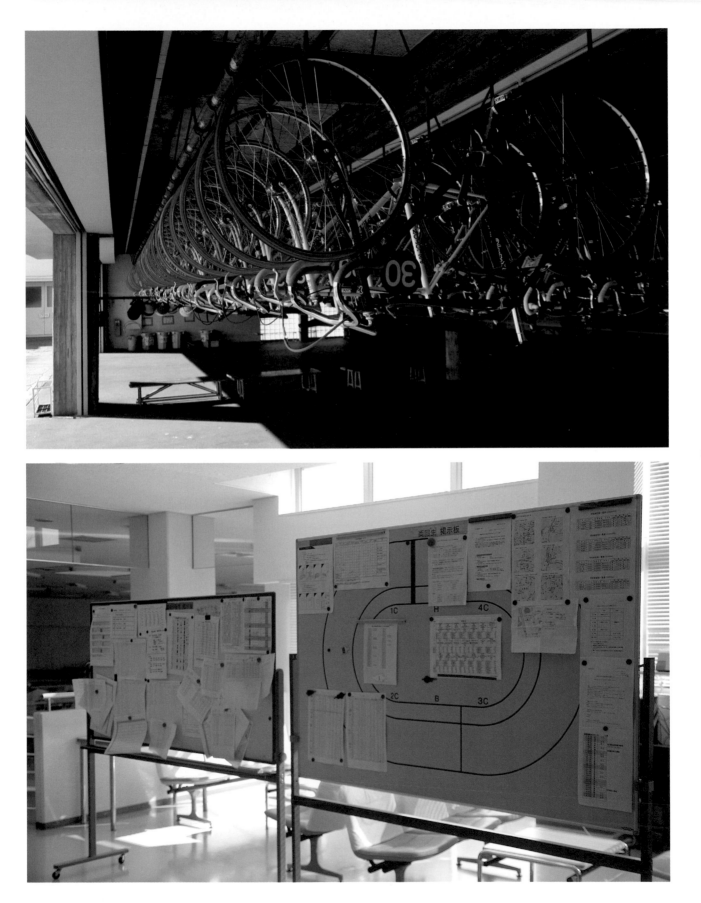

Every year, JKA invites selected international riders, previously including Chris Hoy, Theo Bos and Craig MacLean, to a special summer series that draws huge crowds. 'There are so many rules and betting systems,' says MacLean, who attended Keirin school and competed several times. 'A huge emphasis is put on sticking to your declared tactic and keeping going all the way to the line.' International riders are strong and fast, but suffer from not knowing the rules and underestimating the tactical element of Japanese Keirin. 'The Japanese are so clued up on the rules, they really know how to push the limits. They're good at riding just within them,' Craig says, 'whereas we go out there and make silly mistakes. You don't know what you've done until you've lost 30% of your race winnings as a penalty.' International stars are well paid by JKA, and queue up to attend; conversely, Japanese talent is under-represented on the international stage because Keirin riders are reluctant to leave their lucrative day jobs.

Betting on a Keirin race is both art and science. Lines and tactics are published for punters in advance, but there is also form to consider, blood type and star charts, as well as the riders' relationships and rivalries in each race.

In contrast to these infinite variations, the bikes are subject to strict standards, to prevent any technical advantages that could muddle the odds. Each part must be passed as fit by the JKA and bear the famous NJS stamp. They must also be as robust and as durable as possible, to cope with the stress of racing and minimize accidents that could disrupt the betting or lead to allegations of race-tampering. Besides, no riders want to crash: the track surface is extra-abrasive concrete so that races can continue through all weather conditions. Many competitors are superstitious, sprinkling salt on their bikes for good luck before racing.

Opposite above: A Keirin Grand Prix event – one of the most important events in the calendar – in 2007.

Opposite below: An S-class race.

This page: Newspapers contain statistics about the day's races and riders, helping punters at the races place their bets.

Above: Stratos, a Tokyo-based NJS-certified framebuilder. Complete bicycle courtesy of Tokyo Fixed Gear.

Opposite: Each component, including the chainlinks, is stamped with the NJS logo.

Despite this toughness, Keirin bikes are beautiful, hand-built in steel by craftsmen often in tiny one-man workshops. Some of the master builders apprenticed with classic Italians – Kiyo Miyazawa, for example, studied with Rossin, while Yoshiaki Nagasawa worked under the 'tailor of the bicycle', Sante Pogliaghi and then Ugo De Rosa. Each uses all their skill to make as quick a bike as possible while conforming to NJS regulations. In earlier times, when the tracks were more varied in length and in the angles of their banks, top riders would have bikes made to suit.

Nakano famously rode Nagasawa frames in what is now called 'Nakano red'. 'I helped make the brand famous,' he says, 'and in return the Nagasawa frame helped me achieve my success. I completely trusted him as a builder; it was important just to ride the frame I was given. At my first World Championships I was riding another maker. I asked Nagasawa-san to make me a bike but he wouldn't. About six months later he made me a frame and, when I won the World Championships, Nagasawa-san said he wanted a car. Back then as part of a Keirin prize sometimes you'd get a car. There were around three cyclists using Nagasawa's frames so we promised that the first one to win would give Nagasawa-san a car. I soon won a race and gave him the car. In return, Nagasawa-san said he would build me frames for free for ten years. He later extended this offer until my retirement.'

Opposite: Akio Tanabe shows off the Kalavinka head-badges that his wife paints by hand, as a finishing touch to his NJS-certified frames.

This page, clockwise from right: Outside the one-man workshop; a Kalavinka at Keirin school; Tanabe-san; a vintage Kalavinka being used on the street; unpainted lugs, and bottom bracket shell.

'I've been in the racing world since I was a student. After I graduated in 1974, I went to the World Championships. When I retired, I began making frames. I was taught by a man called Mr Kajiwara, who made my frames when I was racing. That's how I started making frames. Before that I was a test rider for a couple of bicycle manufacturers. During that time I also worked in manufacturing and quality control, so I've been involved with bicycles for over 40 years now.

'I use materials that comply with the NJS standards. When we make a new product we submit the plans and we can only manufacture it when we get approval from NJS. We can use foreign tubing, too, as long as we submit it and get approval. We use tubes made by Columbus or Reynolds, as well as Japanese makes. There are fixed materials and fixed dimensions. Frames that are built within these parameters are NJS standard. It's just like an MOT really: every three years we make a new frame and get it inspected. If it passes then we can use it for another three years as an NJS-approved frame.

'Bicycles are very beautiful objects. But there is a balance to this beauty and it is important to consider this. For example, if the frame is very low but the seatpost is really high then it will not look beautiful.

'The riders I deal with have no off-seasons; they are racing throughout the year. The rider's condition can vary through the seasons; summer, autumn, winter. I try to vary the thickness or the diameter of the pipes and change the angles in the frame.

'I have always built bikes for racers, but I see people ride my bikes in towns these days without any brakes. It's OK to ride on closed roads, but it breaks my heart to see people on bikes with no brakes weaving through pedestrians.'

AKIO TANABE, MASTER BUILDER, KALAVINKA, TOKYO

'It's the equivalent of riding a wild stallion. A donkey, also! The weak in heart aren't going to use it.' Larry Dufus

Previous spread left: Nelson Vails competes at the 1984 Los Angeles Olympics.
Previous spread right: An unknown rider on a Legnano, Fifth Avenue, 1960.
Above: Nelson Vails races for Tempo-Toga as an eighteen-year-old.

In 1984, Nelson Vails, a former New York City messenger, won silver in the individual sprint at the Los Angeles Olympics. Street riding had completed the circle and returned to the track, but first track had to transition to the street.

As in the UK, with its tradition of fixed club riding, there were probably always a few track bike riders on New York's avenues. Some of these guys, now known as the Old Skool Track, would visit the annual Kissena Velodrome flea market and buy cheap old track bikes from the riders. The Italian marques were most treasured: Bottechias, Pinarellos, Cinellis and Frejus, the latter also bought from Tommy Avenia in Spanish Harlem, a fixed aficionado and a major US importer of the marque in the 1960s and 1970s. Then they'd wing their way brakeless through the trucks and buses, on a track gearing with tubs, hopping potholes and developing the street skills that future generations would rely on.

Born in Harlem, Nelson started messengering in 1979, quickly earning his nickname, 'the Cheetah', the fastest cat in the jungle. He didn't ride fixed on the street, because of the racing and training he was doing, but it was around the late 1970s when the first real wave of fixed riders hit the New York streets, immigrants from the Caribbean who began messengering on their track bikes. 'Quite a few guys I worked with had fixed gears; the concept was there,' he says. 'I never

chose to do it, I had two working hand-brakes, and a coaster, how's that? That's how intense I was.'

Larry Dufus is a Jamaican who moved to New York to work as a bike mechanic, before opening his own store, Larry and Jeff's. It's still there today, uptown on Second Avenue, close to its original location. 'I've been here since 1969 and track bikes were a no-no here,' he says. 'Nobody knew about those kind of things – you had to be European or from the Caribbean.'

'Way, way back in Jamaica, they used to have a velodrome in Kingston. In those days – we're talking about 40, 50 years ago – the track bike was the main cycle,' he says. 'Most of the youngsters at that time, that's what they rode.' In 1950s Jamaica the kids rode track bikes to impress the girls and to race, putting together a bike cheaply out of spare parts. 'We used to race for money, and it was really dangerous,' Larry says. 'The races were like a cut-throat thing and people would deliberately knock you over. They'd ride and put out their fingers when they were passing you, and the end of your handlebars would turn around. They'd reach out and touch the end of your handlebar with their fingers. 'Cos it was close. And those days you didn't normally wear helmets until they came out with... I think it was Cinelli. That was the only helmet you'd wear, if you wore one.'

'Shit, guys, I was good. I was fast. I'd jump on an elevator and it would close right in your face, I would beat the light beam, I would slip in, so that by the time the elevator comes back down to get you I've already dropped off my package, I'm on that same elevator.' Nelson Vails

Larry brought his Frejus track bike with him to New York, as did other Caribbean immigrants, who became the city's first track-bike-riding messengers. 'Fast' Eddie Williams hooked up with the Jamaicans and Trinidadians working the streets when he began messengering in 1983. Still a messenger today, he remembers the guys in the early days: 'They were the first,' he says. 'They were there long before I got there, these guys were from the '70s. I was young, I was twenty-two, and these guys paved the way. Track bikes were normal for them.'

In the early 1980s, messengering was at its peak. There were about 7000 messengers working regularly in New York, compared with a quarter that many now. 'It was really good pay then, it was easy,' says Eddie. 'It became a hobby, then turned into a career. The company I worked for, the base rate was $9.50, so you got half. You worked five days straight, you got 60%. After tax you came home with good money to live off back then. You could find a nice loft apartment in Williamsburg for cheap; now you can't.'

'This was way before the fax machine,' says Nelson. 'There was a major demand in a place like New York City, where people need things NOW. I hit it at its peak. Now you have emails, so people don't use messengers as much, but when I was doing it people used messengers for anything and everything.' Nelson reckoned on doing 35-60 drops a day and got the high-value jobs because of his speed, always making 60 cents on the dollar. 'I was one of the top ten messengers in New York City, time-wise.' he says. 'I was reliable. Most guys won't work if it's raining, but I'll have my rain jacket on and I'm gone. I had the ear of the dispatchers because it could be raining at 8am and I'm calling in at 7:59.'

'You lock your legs and you manoeuvre the bike, you control the bike, because if the bike controls you...'
Eddie Williams

Below: Squid, shot by Eddie Williams.

Cruising fixed with one of the New York old skool is intense. Riding the yellow line, slipping through currents of traffic, uptown on Sixth, back down on Fifth, running red lights, threading through pedestrians and cross-town traffic to make it through. Banging on vans and trailing fingers along the side of buses in sight of the driver's mirror - to let them know you're there, as a talisman against their power to crush you without missing a rev.

'Anything goes, and everyone's fighting for space, trying to squeeze in and get past,' says Squid, a messenger who started in the early 1990s and is now a partner at Cyclehawk Messengers Inc. 'I always treat people with respect. I think that anyone who's out there, we're all playing the same game; if you're all paying attention you can avoid just about anything. I've been in situations where I've made mistakes and a cab driver has fast reflexes and not hit me, so I can't say I hate anyone... they drive crazily and so do I. You just have to stay focused and pay attention.'

'I don't know of anyone who got hit by cars in my era,' says Nelson, 'but guys who get hit get hit because they're not focusing on their situation. I stayed focused on what was going to happen, what you could expect to happen; you could see at a distance someone getting ready to flag a cab, and you could see the cab on your left peripheral, and you know that he's gonna cross the street all the way and he may not see you. So you gotta see him. You gotta expect that.'

If you catch the lights right on one of the great north-south avenues, and are spinning at something over 20mph (32kmh), you can ride without hitting a red for 30, 40 blocks or more. 'It seems like New York was almost built for riding track bikes. You can flow and catch waves of green lights and go and go and go for miles,' says Squid. 'It's something I haven't really found in other cities - except Mexico City, which has huge long avenues like that. In most cities, the streets get broken up a lot more.'

Riding track isn't just fun; for messengers it is also a good tool for the job. 'The cool thing about track bikes is there's not a lot of stuff to take care of,' says Squid. 'You don't have to worry about the derailleur, the shifter cables and all that stuff. When it's raining and snowing, and there's a lot of dirt in the city, that really runs that stuff down quickly, so if you don't have any cables it's easier to take care of your bike.'

'Back then, track bikes took over. If it wasn't a track bike it was a fixed gear, a road bike turned fixed,' says Eddie. 'That was the scene, that was the only scene. They were faster and easier to manoeuvre in traffic, it was easier to brake with your legs than your hands. I think the whole community adapted to track bikes. We used to go to Enoch's in Hell's Kitchen, he used to sell these bikes called Matsuris. They were old, and cheaply made in Japan, but they were really nice, they were strong, they were made for messengers. Every messenger I knew had a Matsuri. They became legendary.'

Below: Fast Eddie Williams poses with his Matsuri for a photoshoot in the 1980s.

For Nelson, life revolved around messengering and racing, which he didn't take too seriously at first: 'I was having fun, just having fun racing. I enjoyed kicking your ass at the weekends, partying Friday night, Saturday morning. I'd come in and have a bowl of Wheaties an hour before I head to the start line and kick your ass, then go have breakfast with my buddies. Those were the good old days. Me and Born, my childhood friend, would do the messenger thing, party till five in the morning at some house party club – today they call them raves. Six in the morning, I'm on the start line, I win 50 bucks, then go take all my buddies from that party the night before out to breakfast. They're all waiting for me, so I had to win, it was one of those pressure things – like, "You'd better win us some money, because you're buying breakfast." That was the motivational goal.'

Later, Nelson raced seriously, as Pan-American champion and at the Olympics, then professionally on the European six-day circuit and in Japan, but he never quite left his messengering days behind. 'This whole messenger thing, being raised in New York City, with a New York mentality... that mentality helped my whole cycling career as far as awareness for racing on the track and knowing what I was doing – especially as a sprinter, in a tactical game. I was able not to put myself in any predicament because of my messenger work. A mass start race on the track, it's like being in New York City downtown, with a bunch of cars and cabs, same concept, so you just don't allow yourself to get into a jam.'

Above: Mo, who later opened the Keirin Cycle Culture Café in Berlin, phones in for a job in New York, 2002. Right: A present-day New York messenger.

'There's a certain kind of pride in not having a brake, but it also makes you rely more on the skill of riding that way – if you have a brake, you don't have to really commit to that style of riding.' Squid

The messenger community today is global, but back in the 1980s and early 1990s horizons were more limited. Many in New York, when they started out, didn't know the city beyond their own borough. 'I used to be a walking messenger. I used to walk and take the train until some friends said, "Hey man, buy a bike",' says Eddie Williams. 'Most people from New York had never been to Midtown, or the West Village, they were from Brooklyn, or uptown. Numbers is no problem, but in SoHo, in the West Village, you got names.' Nevertheless, the community was there. 'It was the most beautiful thing I ever saw in my life. After we finished work we would all get together in Washington Square Park. That's how you knew there were so many bikers. We came from all over.'

In 1993, the first Cycle Messenger World Championships were held in Berlin. The event brought messengers together to race, testing their bike skills, speed and navigation, their ability to work under pressure. Buffalo Bill was a London cycle courier at the time: 'In terms of physically meeting, that was it,' he says. 'When we went to the first CMWC in '93, we sort of knew the East Coast guys in America were riding fixies because I'd corresponded with people in New York, and I'd seen this comic, called *Messenger 29*, written by Jay Jones in 1989. In that you can see the guy's riding a fixie,' says Bill. 'In '93, I was riding a fixie – Andy Capp's fixie. Eric Zo was riding a fixie, one Berliner was riding a fixie, who everyone in Berlin thought was weird... Steve and Eric from DC, that was it. Everyone else was riding road bikes or street mountain bikes. It was broadly speaking Europeans there, but there were some Americans.'

London hosted the following year, and 1995, in Toronto, was when North America turned up for the first time en masse. 'It was mental, just heaps of people,' remembers Bill. 'Everyone was getting naked and there was a mass naked ride one night. That was a Boston thing. At one point there were about 100 people totally naked riding down Queen Street. The weekend after, there was a massive alleycat.' Toronto was Squid's first CMWC. 'That's when I realized, wow, these people hang out and they do stuff together, and they race,' he says, 'I was pretty naïve. I thought I was going to win, but I ended up not even qualifying. It inspired me to come back to New York and throw an alleycat three months later. At first I wanted to get people together for a fun, positive thing. Also, I love just going fast.'

Left: The start of an alleycat race in New York.
Below: *Messenger 29*, from September Press.

71

Above: A Western Union messenger, New York, 1896.

Right: *Critérium des Porteurs de Journaux* race in the streets of Paris, 1941.

London's first alleycat was in 1994 and, by Toronto 1995, messenger races were nothing new. After all, there had been cycle messengers in the US since the nineteenth century, when the Western Union boys ruled the city streets. 'There's a great picture from 1896 of a brakeless fixed-gear Western Union messenger in New York – it looks like he could bar-spin and everything' says Squid. 'I can just imagine those guys getting their 75-cent paycheck at the end of the week and being like, "Yo, first one to Battery Park gets the other one's paycheck".'

Modern alleycats – unsanctioned, often impromptu street races that mimic a messenger's daily work by involving navigation, checkpoints and pick-ups – were born in Toronto in the mid-1980s, and the first race named an alleycat was contested for Halloween 1989. In form, they closely resemble the annual *Critérium des Porteurs de Journaux*, which ran in Paris from 1895 until the 1960s, pitting newspaper boys in a race for glory on the city's cobbled streets. Many of the newspaper *porteurs* were good amateur racers; paid by the drop, they used their speed and strength to sprint from the printing press to the newspaper kiosks several times a day, earning more than their bosses or the paper's top executives. In the *Critérium* they raced their single-speed bikes – the best custom-made by France's finest constructeurs – laden with 15kg (33lb) of newspapers, which they had to exchange at a half-way checkpoint.

Above: Berlin alleycat.
Opposite (top to bottom, left to right): A checkpoint in an alleycat race; performing tasks in an alleycat; skidding, New York City; messengers race in Zurich; a cargo bike race; Fast Friday, Seattle; Sino, CMWC champion 2008, at Kyotoloco 2005.

Monster Track, a New York race started in 2000 run predominantly for messengers by a messenger named Snake, is the best-known track-bike-only alleycat. 'I'd been to an all-brakeless alleycat before Monster Track, at the world championships in 1996 in San Francisco,' says Squid. 'There were a ton of brakeless riders showing up for that, a lot of messengers from New York and Boston, Philadelphia and DC. That event spread it a lot to the West Coast. They saw the style and couldn't believe the guys were bombing the hills, even though it was kinda crazy, but people were handling their rides. Even back then it was spreading through those type of events.'

'Cycle racing for women is generally acknowledged to be undesirable,' said Frederick Bidlake, the inventor of the time trial, in an invective from 1912. 'My ideal of a clever lady rider is one who can ride far, who can ride at a really useful speed, who mounts hills with comfort, and makes no fuss or show of effort. The stylish, clever lady stops short of being a scorcher.' Now we've got over his chauvinism, women are messengering and participating in alleycats the world over.

Opposite above: Fixed riders in Taipei. Opposite below, left: Unorthodox parking as fixies take over among Milan's younger riders. Opposite below, right: A Fast Friday meet in Seattle. Started by Dustin Klein (pictured, with megaphone), the night became a focus for the city's track bike riders and was profiled in 2008 in a documentary of the same name.

77

As informal events, run by people who generally don't like rules, often on busy city streets, alleycats hold inherent dangers. Many devotees are content for them to remain underground, and unpublicized, open only to the most skilful riders. Nonetheless, alleycats now happen the world over, contested by messengers, their friends and urban riders, usually on fixed, and CMWCs now contain subsidiary, fixed-specific events, including longest-skid and track-standing

competitions. In 2008, Sino of Tokyo was the first messenger to win CMWC (in Toronto again) riding fixed and without a hand-brake, beating two other fixed riders into second and third places. Not, as Buffalo Bill writes in *Moving Target Messenger Zine*, 'that this proves the superiority of fixies over free. I think it simply proves that fixies are popular amongst messengers'.

San Francisco may be one of the
most unlikely places for track bikes to
flourish, yet on the city's hills, street riding
is reaching one of its ultimate forms of
expression. Mash SF, a group of riders from
across San Francisco's cycling community
first showed the city's track-bike potential
to the world. Macaframa, another, newer,
collective of riders, have now also released
a film, combining skate-video style and
cinematic techniques.

Travis T, a former messenger, now proprietor
of the Freewheel Bike Shop on Hayes, has
watched things progress. 'When I first
moved here in '94, there were only three
or four messengers riding track bikes,' he
says. 'They'd hang out downtown on their
downtime, doing tricks down at the Wall,
just killing time between deliveries – goofing
off and trying to ride backwards. That
seemed like it was the beginning of it all.'

79

**'A track bike in a city just makes sense.
To get around a city, it's perfect. It's fucking fast, quiet and
allows for a true riding experience to happen.'**
Mike and Gabe, Mash SF

'Back in '94 there was a place downtown called The Fixed Gear. They didn't have any fixed-gear parts, it was just the name of the shop. I asked my friend Joel when I started messengering where to find parts and he said: "Oh, it's funny, if you go to The Fixed Gear, they don't have any fixed-gear parts, but if you go to The Freewheel they have fixed-gear parts".'

As with other cities, it was messengers who brought track bikes to the streets, yet many chose to ride geared because of the hills. 'There are some who do courthouse filings, riding to the courthouse over and over again, so riding track bikes isn't a problem,' says Travis. 'Then there are other guys riding all over the city doing long tags, on commission. A lot of those guys don't ride track bikes because they're really hustling around the city and they couldn't get it done as quickly. A couple of them still do, though, which is amazing.'

The hills pose as many opportunities as difficulties. Just over the Golden Gate Bridge, in Marin County, they gave birth to the mountain bike; similarly, the city's slopes have bred a new way of thinking about how to ride a track bike. A rider skidding in graceful turns down California Street resembles a snowboarder or skateboarder choosing a line down a hill.

'I think many of us have been involved in the skateboard industry or have skateboarded in the past, or still skateboard,' says Garrett Chow, a Mash SF rider. 'That comes across when you see certain people – the way they read traffic or the way they ride in traffic is really an extension of their skateboard background, you can see it in their riding style.' Colby Elrick, co-director of the Macaframa movie, cut his teeth filming skating: 'With a track bike you do it yourself, like on a skateboard,' he says. 'You gotta push your ass everywhere, you don't have gears to do it for you. You can do powerslides on your bike, whip skids – basically the same as skating. Most importantly, you can bomb hills.'

Steve Brezovec, a Macaframa rider, also sees a similar attraction in board sports and riding track on the hills: 'I used to do a lot of downhill skateboarding, and it's like that but faster. I also still snowboard a lot, I do technical steep chutes. Stuff where you can't stop and you just have to have good control in the chute – and you can't fall really, or you'll slide to the bottom and die! I think a lot of it is just nerves: it's about keeping your focus and your attitude together. Like when you go really fast and you have to split between a couple of cars. It's about trying to stay cool.' When asked about the parallels with snowboarding, Colin Arlen, co-director of Macaframa, just chuckles: 'Just go as fast as possible and avoid anything and everything in your path – like a car is a tree, a moving tree.'

There is a strong cycling counterculture in the Bay area, epitomized by shops like Montano Velo and the East Bay Mice riders. However, it remained underground until Mash SF started posting short video clips to the internet, which became the basis for the Mash SF film from 2007. 'We wanted to capture what was happening in San Francisco from 2004 to 2007,' explain Mike Martin and Gabe Morford, the film's directors. 'When we started we knew all 18 riders who used a track bike on the street for work, or transportation, and a few of them were pushing what was possible on these bikes. In the video we were simply letting the riding speak for itself. We would get out all the time, but the camera was not the focus for being on the bike. The sense of community was really strong because we felt like this small group that knew about this secret... we just wanted to ride.'

Rainier Schaefer, Macaframa and Mash rider.

On a fundamental level, a track bike – built for travelling horizontally – seems absurd here, but the adrenaline is worth it. Ride a San Francisco hill and your legs know it. Up, and you're straining, even on a 65" gear (although most riders choose 49/17 or 49/18); down and you're spinning out, testing the integrity of chain, tyres, muscle and sinew, popping skids, playing chicken with your fear as gravity pulls you ever faster. As Gabe and Mike say: 'A brakeless track bike on the street is a death wish. You did not get into it because it was simple, it was because you needed to face, and to some degree conquer, this challenge. To do it in SF is no different than in New York, Chicago, LA, or any other dense city. They all have their unique aspect, and San Francisco's is clearly the hills. You learn your lines – what you like, what routes you take – and these change as your ability changes. Do you wiggle, or do you climb Haight? Do you wiggle, or drop Oak?'

Above: Big Red of Macaframa on Duncan Street.

Opposite above: Phil, Macaframa.

Opposite below, from left: Garrett, Demarco and James of Mash, and a pile of used tyres lying by the road.

'Those skaters brought stuff to a whole other level. They had a whole different mindset that came from looking at how to skate terrain... y'know, now they're at the same spot on a track bike and thinking, what can I do here?'

Travis T, Freewheel

The city is a playground that forces riders to hone their skills and their style. The Macaframa crew came together after Mash SF; their film, like Mash's, is a love letter to San Francisco, its topography and character. 'Riding track on the street lets you exhibit good judgement and foresight, as well as your manoeuvring and handling abilities,' says Phil Cheng. 'In traffic, it's fun to see an obstacle before you and plan what to do if it does something hurtful to you. And if it actually does happen, and you do what you forethought, it's very gratifying. To be able to stop on a dime on a bike without brakes is very enjoyable, particularly on the hills of San Francisco. Being capable of managing yourself down these hills safely, efficiently and, moreover, stylishly, is also very gratifying.'

'I think what keeps me riding,' says Rainier Schaefer, another Macaframa rider who also rides with Mash, 'is simply getting across the city: knowing that there's a mountain between point A and point B and it might be faster to go over it, or it might be faster to stick to the major thoroughfares around it. It's really fun to beat cars and make lights... or not make lights and run them, whatever. A week ago I was coming down Alamonte – you can make the lights for about a mile – spinning out, really just having a good time. I come up to an intersection and, about four cars back from where they were stopped, do a skid, then do another one, and then I'm coasting. I fully put my foot on the tire and stop before the intersection... and my chain had just fucking popped off! It was really terrifying. I mean, if I'd

had a brake it'd have been real easy to stop it, no problem. But then I wouldn't be in Macaframa.'

Macaframa rules say no brakes allowed, and many of the riders keep their bikes track-pure, with drops, and no concessions to roadworthiness. 'I think that would diminish the fun of it,' says Phil. 'We like riding track bikes because of the steepness of the geometry and the twitchy handling that affords. To compromise that feeling would be to compromise the essence of the fun-ness of these bicycles.'

'There are people that ride track bikes on the street and then there are people who ride fixed gears,' says Colby. 'Real track bikes shouldn't have brakes drilled for them,' continues Colin. 'If you're going to ride a real track bike, you should ride it without a brake. You should learn to ride your bike the way it's meant to ride.'

Below: Emi, Mash.

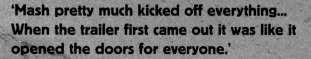

'Mash pretty much kicked off everything... When the trailer first came out it was like it opened the doors for everyone.'
Andy Ellis, Fixed Gear London

'I don't think moustache bars have ever gone that fast in the history of mankind...'
Garrett Chow

Opposite: John Igei of Mash.

Above: Garrett, Rainier and Mash riders in Austen, Texas with Lance Armstrong.

Below: Garrett and Walton shadow the Tour of California, 2009.

'People are exploring the limitations of the bike, really trying to push it, which is good,' says Colin. 'But you should pick and choose what you want to adapt for the new workspace of the track bike. There are certain tricks that transcend all niches of biking, like wheelies, but we've tried to make sure that somebody who's in Macaframa knows how to ride their bike hard and fast, and tricks are more of a secondary thing, a natural thing that comes out of the riding.'

'Our hearts are on the street,' say Gabe and Mike. 'So we hope to continue to create video shorts in this vein. If we let that be a jump-off for all things cycling, then we will continue to do it for the right reasons.' The Mash and Macaframa films capture pure, indefinable experience. The feeling of spinning madly down a hill, taking cars on the outside, running lights - a savage grace of movement, the freedom of unreasonable speed. 'We filmed almost from a spectator's standpoint,' says Colin. 'Like if you were to see somebody fly down the street and pan your head with them. And then they're gone.'

Opposite: Parts on display, W-Base, Shibuya. Above: 'Pisto' bikes and ramen, Shinbashi. Rider: Kouta.

Step off any one of Tokyo's major roads, and you delve into a maze of narrow streets without names; each area, partitioned by four-lane highways, a tight jumble of buildings and styles old and new – a hundred small cities within one big one.

Shibuya and Harajuku are the spiritual home of the track bike in the city. Shibuya houses Carnival, one of the original track bike boutiques, as well as W-Base, a BMX-slash-track shop which, in typical Tokyo style, is squeezed in on the ground floor of the same building. Harajuku, meanwhile, is the crucible of Japanese street style. As with many other underground trends that weren't invented in Japan, track-bike culture has been obsessively taken up by a select few, mostly after Mash SF visited Tokyo for the first time in 2006. Hiroshi Fujiwara, designer, DJ and 'King of Harajuku', attended a screening of the Mash SF film and a cult was born.

Above: Disc wheel by ESOW, trispoke by KAMI. Below and overleaf: Crime is rare, so track bikes can be left almost unlocked in Tokyo's parks and streets.

Fujiwara collects old British frames, including a jewel-studded Hetchins, whereas Carnival sells mainly vintage Italian bikes. Most people, however, make do with NJS cast-offs from the Keirin circuit – although prices have gone up and good frames are scarcer as interest in NJS parts explodes in the West. On conspicuous display in the streets is a rainbow of NJS frames, with Deep Vs, Aerospokes, Heds, disc wheels, risers and every imaginable modification, making Japan the home of street customization. There is an infinite number of variations on a theme, reflecting the more limited diversity of Keirin bikes within the conformity of the NJS standards.

Japanese cycle couriers did ride fixed before it became more widely popular, but the track bike is not as ubiquitous as in New York or London, perhaps due to Tokyo's size and the area a messenger must cover. Hal and Sino are two of the city's most respected messengers. 'I prefer things that are analogue,' says Sino, CMWC Champion 2008. 'I think high-tech bikes are cool too, but as a messenger I think fixed-gear bikes are nicer to ride. My job is an analogue job, after all.' Hal agrees: 'When I started riding fixed there were only two or three others in Tokyo who were riding fixed. I didn't really know what I was doing; I just ended up buying a fixed-gear bike and having a go. I like the simplicity of it: when you pedal forwards you move forwards. Pedal backwards and you go backwards. It's as if it's a part of my body.'

'There is no particular reason I ride fixed really. It's like fancying a girl. It was just like, hmmmm, that's nice!' Hal

A fixed gear is practical for the job, but Sino also admits to being influenced by other messengers around the world. 'It is easier to maintain a fixed-gear bike,' he says, 'but about five

Above: Hal's custom Amanda frame, with protest brake.
Below: An NJS frame broken by tricks riding.

'I was in New York waiting for a red light and this old man said to me, "You're a messenger right? Then why are you waiting for the red light?" In my view it's more important for messengers not to harm other people than not break the law.' Sino

years ago when we started riding fixed it was much more rare; that's why we all got into it, really. When I saw foreign books on messengers, like *Messengers Style*, it felt like if you were a messenger then fixed-gear bikes were what you should be riding.'

Some Tokyo courier companies discourage or even ban their riders from riding fixed. Others insist that their employees fit a brake. Clamp-on Keirin training brakes are sometimes used, but often messengers – it not being a profession that attracts conformists – disobey by fitting the brake lever in an impractical position where it is technically operable but deliberately useless.

Sino's Kalavinka has a brake lever yet no cable connecting it to the calliper. For him, it's an important sign of his mastery of the bike. 'The fastest messengers in the world have no brakes, and I want to be on the same level as them,' he says. 'No handicaps. I just became world champion this year but, for example, if I had been using brakes and the second or third rider was riding brakeless then I'd think that was much more hardcore.'

For the rest of the population, heavy bicycles with step-through frames – *Mamacharis* ('mother's bikes'), usually black – are the traditional mode of transport, weaving through the pedestrians on the city's pavements. As a result, Japanese drivers are unused to making allowances for bikes on the road, especially those ridden fast. And, explains Hal, 'In Japan there is no culture to protect cyclists. In Japan cyclists are considered to be weak and everybody hates cyclists. Cars hate bicycles and pedestrians hate bicycles!'

The messenger's job is further complicated by Tokyo's lack of street names or signs. Each district has a name, and within that district there are numbered areas. The irregularly shaped blocks have numbers and the buildings are numbered on each block, but often in no discernible order. Addresses can be difficult, if not impossible, to locate, and the labyrinthine layout means that even locals and messengers can get lost in a district they know well. 'Tokyo has to be one of the most difficult cities to courier in. Only the big streets have names,' says Hal. 'It's pretty different from other cities outside of Japan. If you don't have a map you will never find the place. The roads in Tokyo aren't in a grid like Kyoto so it's a very complicated city. You have to have a sixth sense!'

Meanwhile, in parks across the city, the tricks scene is exploding. Keirin bikes are not up to the heavy-duty punishment they get from a tricks rider – and many second-hand NJS frames are only on the market because they have been raced and crashed, and are therefore fragile. Tokyo's tricks riders prefer newer alloy bikes, Vigorellis and Pista Concepts, and the street-fixed Gangsta Track sells more quickly than Brooklyn Machine Works can import them.

Toku, wall ride, Tokyo.

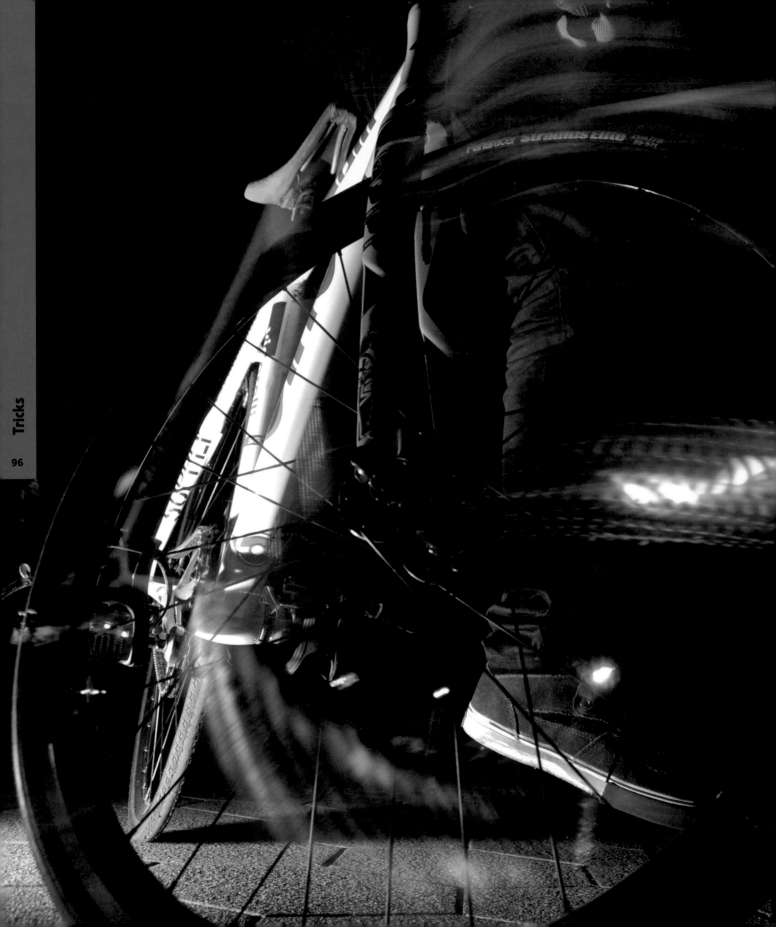

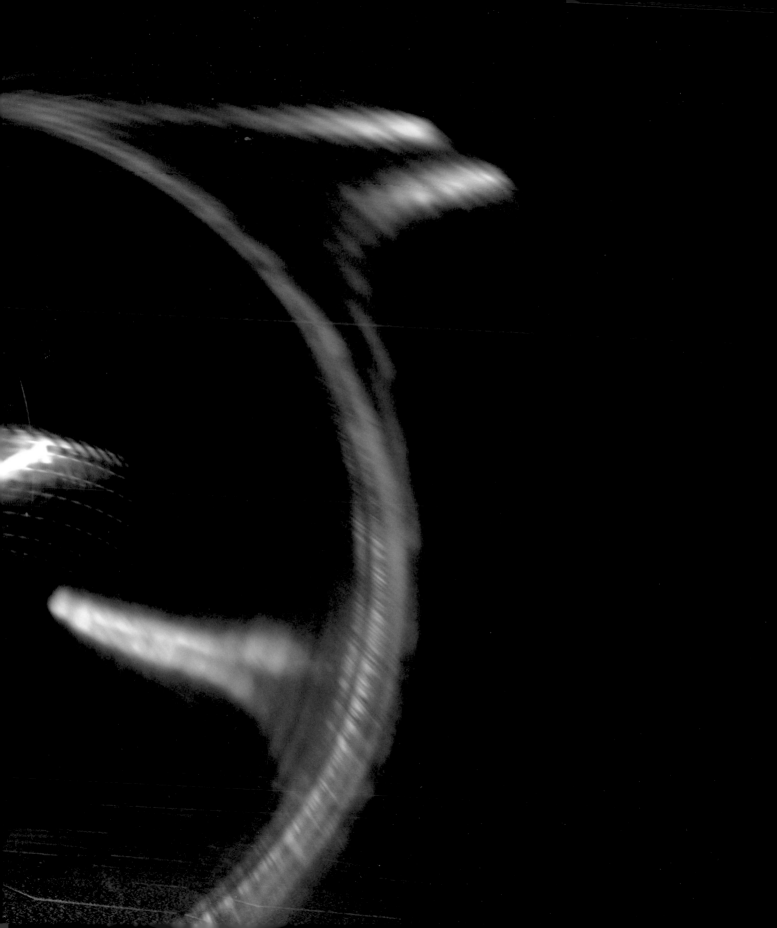

Most track bikes today never see the inside of a velodrome. Street riding is already at one remove from its intended purpose, and many who love the motion and challenge of a fixed gear often change tyres and rims, or fit a brake, to make their bikes more road-worthy.

As their use evolves and multiplies, bike design is changing. Skid tricks are the natural first progression but, as SuperTed of Fixed Gear London says, 'People come to tricks on fixed gear from different backgrounds, coming from a different angle.' New generations of riders, less influenced by messengers, are approaching their bikes in a different way. In Seattle, says Colin Arlen of Macaframa, 'you have the messengers who work hard and ride their bikes all day long, then you have these other kids who are coming from this hip generation influenced by YouTube. It's spawned this present-day culture of riding and riders. They skipped a certain level of tricks, a certain level of riding, and they went straight to wheelies and Keo-esque tricks.'

Above and right: Phil Cheng, Macaframa.

Above: Tokyo.
Below: SuperTed jumps a gap.

'A lot of people are doing tricks on bikes, breaking stuff; you need to make bikes better for the purpose.'
SuperTed, Fixed Gear London

The internet and projects like the Bootleg Sessions videos have created a global community pushing tricks riding forward. 'You see someone and think, I can do that, or do something different, and it just progresses,' says SuperTed. Riders on flatland are developing levels of control on a par with circus riders, and fixed gears are now going down stairs, over jumps, up walls, things that looked impossible even a year ago. 'It's more of a challenge than a BMX, because the fixed gear means you have to think more of the timing,' says SuperTed, although Andy Ellis, co-founder of Fixed Gear London, disagrees: 'I don't see it like that. I've never ridden BMX, so I find it impossible to do tricks on a BMX, or even a mountain bike. I find it easier because you have more control. I've never wheelied before but on a fixed gear I can.'

'It's definitely not a traditional track bike, but then again no one's riding track bikes in a traditional way, so it makes sense.'
Joe Avedisian, Brooklyn Machine Works

Right: The Gangsta Track is particularly popular in Japan among tricks riders. Below: The workshop at Powers Street, Brooklyn, New York, where all the Brooklyn Machine Works bikes are built by hand.

The Brooklyn Machine Works workshop on Powers Street in Williamsburg makes around 400 frames a year; the majority are Gangsta Tracks, designed for street fixed and trick riding. 'It's just like freestyle was in BMX days,' says the brand's founder, Joe Avedisian. 'You can hang out, there's always an empty lot somewhere, it just requires your bike.' He learnt his framebuilding in London, in the basement of Yellow Jersey cycles, and had the idea for the Gangsta Track in the 1980s, when New York's first wave of fixed messengers hit. Its design, however, was influenced by his first track bike, a vintage Raleigh that still hangs from a rack above the workshop floor.

'The geometry of the Gangsta Track is heavily influenced by the geometry of the track bikes of the mid-1960s. Bikes were a little bit longer, more relaxed, so on the streets they feel a lot better,' he says, 'We have a lot of cool people giving input on geometry, how a bike feels or rides. What's interesting about the Gangsta Track is how good it does at alleycats as well as freestyle. Tom Lamarche is breaking doors open on the level of tricks and stuff, then we've got Austin Horse, who just won the North American Cycle Courier Championships.'

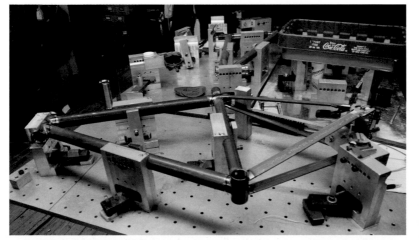

Opposite, below: Tom LaMarche rides around the world in Paris. This page: Keo Curry does his signature trick, the Keo spin.

Supercharged by the internet, it is impossible to predict where fixed tricks will go from here. It seems, however, that a certain level of elegance and refinement will carry over from the era of true track bikes, the gnarly drops and stunts tempered by the control of the fixed gear.

'I think people will start doing simple tricks again, stop trying to combine everything into one, so it looks good and it looks really fluid,' says Colby Elrick. BMX companies are developing fixed-specific frames, showing that more BMX riders are entering the scene, but, for Joe, something essential about the bikes will remain: 'We've talked about making an even more trick-oriented track bike. Ours are definitely some of the best suited for that kind of riding, but I think it's limited because the bikes are so simple - how far can you go with it? We're already pushing the envelope of acceptability with a longer fork, the wheelspan and the sloping top tube. People are having a hard time accepting that.'

'I've never ridden in
a city like London,' says Eric
Von Munz, a long-time messenger from
Milwaukee. 'London's got a lot of cities beat,
just in terms of volume and tightness – you've got
your shoulder on the centre-line, and that's it.'

London, although congested and dangerous, is increasingly a
cyclist's city. The transformation noticeably gathered pace when
the terrorist attacks in July 2007 forced people off public transport
– whether out of choice or necessity – and on to their bikes. Before
that, however, change was slow. In the 1980s, nobody cycled, and
fixed riders, says Buffalo Bill, a courier for over a decade who still
runs *Moving Target*, were at the very fringes of the fringe. 'When
you rode fixed-wheel then, you'd get people telling you, "Your
knees are going to blow off," or "Isn't it really dangerous
with the kerbs?" People our age thought we were
mental. The only people who were positive about
it were old men, because it was totally
natural to them,' he says.

   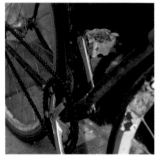

Above: Riders on the londonfgss.com Tweed Run, January 2009.

Bill bought his first fixed in the mid-1980s from a
friend, Andy Capp, maybe the first courier in London
to ride fixed, and became one of only five who did
so. 'There were a couple of guys riding who were
club cyclists, who were really in the minority. The
rest of us, we'd taken up cycling because we were
messengers. We had no idea about the club scene,
or training on fixed wheels in the winter.' Bill is also
sure that the London fixed riders were not imitating
their US counterparts. After all, it's nothing new
on British roads, and in a sense part of the cycling
establishment. 'I was on the *Today* programme
with John Humphrys,' says Bill. 'He was talking to
me before we went on air and asked, "So, when I
was a kid in the '50s, we rode these things called
fixed wheels, do people still ride them?"' It really
took over among messengers, Bill says, in around
2003, which is also the year that some, following
the example of continental messengers visiting for
the European Messenger Championships, started
removing their front brakes.

'Oxford Street's a blast, I had a blast.'
Eric Von Munz, writer, Cog Magazine

Both pages: Stills from Brunelle's helmet-cam video shot during the London Calling alleycat in 2006.

'Riding here is different from other cities, in the sense that if you go to other cities like New York the roads are much wider,' says Bill. 'I think that's why those guys ride brakeless. Those guys have a lot more room; you run out of road a lot more quickly here. If you're going to ride properly fast you need a front brake. But what do I know... That's the thing about London for me; it's a really claustrophobic city, there isn't a lot of room anywhere. That's what makes the bridges really special - that's the only time you see the sky.'

London is a mess: complicated and twisty. 'It's like somebody just laid down a bunch of pixie sticks and said, "OK, that's where the roads go",' says Eric. 'But Oxford Street, as hairy as it is, is a pretty good route, it's a pretty standard artery.'

For some Londoners this is all part of the appeal. 'The good thing about London is it's so intricate and tight, and you don't know what's coming round the corner,' says Andy Ellis

of Fixed Gear London. 'Whereas when we rode in Paris, it's all big roads, cycle lanes and massive junctions. If you go across a junction you're risking your life, because it's about six lanes of traffic - you can't get through that! Here it's two or four, max.'

Fixed Gear London is a diverse collective that coalesced around the bike and who have become world-renowned for their riding. But although London makes for good riding, it's difficult to replicate the experience. 'We're trying to film at the moment and it's so hard,' says Andy. 'You have to be on another bike, a fixed gear and even then you can't take the same chances the person in front takes... but that's what will make it good, too. That's why there aren't many films from London. If you go out on a motorbike, people have to give you room, and then it's not real.'

440 YDS.

TRIBUNE CYCLE METER

OUR LAPS TO A MILE.

YDS. 220

THE TRIBUNE BLUE STREAK.

Photo by Horner Boston COPYRIGHT 1901

Mile a minute Murphy and Tom Butler

Top: Reg Harris, Britain's number one rider in the '50s, beats his arch rival Arie van Vliet to the line.

Above and left: Eddie Wingrave rides the rollers in his heyday.

Opposite: Charles 'Mile-a-Minute' Murphy races Tom Butler in 1901. Murphy was the first man to ride a bicycle one mile in less than a minute. He achieved this in a specially constructed aerodynamic shield behind a train on the Long Island Rail Road, covering the distance in 57.8 seconds, in 1899.

Rollers have been used since cycling's early days as a warm-up and training tool, and for competitive events in their own right: two or more rollers are placed side by side, linked to a giant dial with two hands showing each bike's progress. The first person to a set distance - now usually 500 or 1000m - wins. In the 1940s and 1950s, roller racing was a real crowd-puller. Eddie Wingrave, one of the era's greats, remembers it well. He worked for Freddie Grubb, a London shop-owner and framebuilder who sold dozens of rollers to Mecca; Eddie toured bingo palaces and dance halls around the country, accompanied by bands and dancers, promoting roller races on television and taking on local hotshots keen to challenge one of Britain's best riders.

'It must have been in '51. Reg Harris was number one, I was number two at that time,' says Eddie. 'Grimsby, we opened up there, and I rode on top of a taxi. We fixed the rollers on top of a taxi and I rode on top of it, in the market square, just as an advert.' Then, in the evenings, Eddie would race, while the compère hyped the crowds. 'We'd invite the audience on to the bikes - they were bolted to the rollers so they couldn't fall off. You'd go to the local clubs, get them to come along, then go to the local dealer and get him to present prizes. I used to get telegraph boys out to ride, because they were strong,' explains Eddie. 'I never had many serious challengers, but there was one in Liverpool, a lad who was a serious rider. He did 70mph and I had to go after him, I had to do him. The bandmaster was the timekeeper, and he had a list of times and the speeds. When I went on I did 72mph. I had to beat him! That was the showmanship, you know. At Liverpool, the Shakespeare it was, the stagehands almost walked out because there were so many people backstage who wanted to ride.'

Eddie rode on TV, and at the Albert Hall during cycling concerts and the British Best All Rounder competition. He even remembers legendary Italian *campionissimo* Fausto Coppi taking a spin: 'Coppi was there for the Cycling Diamond Jubilee, and I was the only one allowed on stage... he wouldn't fly then, and we had to get him to Victoria Station at 9 o'clock to get the train home.'

Somewhere along the line, roller racing fell out of fashion, as did the dance halls, and it was forgotten until messengers at CMWC 1999 in Zurich stumbled upon the third annual Goldsprint competition in the city's TurbinenBräu brewery. Founded by local brewer and cyclist, Tony Weber, and named after one of his beer brands, the combination of beer and cycling couldn't fail to excite. Within a few months, roller races were back on the bill in New York and London, revived in the UK by Greg Tipper. This legacy was taken on by other messengers, Caspar Hughes and Paul 'Winston' Churchill, who run Rollapaluza today.

Rollapaluza now brings the same combination of showmanship and brute physical effort to cities across the UK. The atmosphere is intense. MCs and showgirls hype the crowd, pounding music keeps the cadence up, competitors sweat, strain and gurn in battle. Some of the greatest cyclists in Britain have ridden the Rollapaluza rollers, including Chris Hoy (on his first 'competitive' ride after the Beijing Olympics), Craig MacLean, Dave Le Grys and Lee Povey. Different sets of rollers are not comparable: some give faster times than others depending on diameter, rolling resistance and other factors, but times on the Rollapaluza competition rollers and standard 44/14 gearing have plummeted to previously unimaginable levels. Craig MacLean held the record of 18.94 seconds until Matt Crampton, one of the rising stars of Team GB, blew it out of the water in February 2009. He rode 500m in 17.90 seconds, 62.8mph at an average of 254rpm.

Above and opposite: Rollapaluza, 2007-8.
Below: Goldsprints, New York City.

There's little raw power involved – a good time on the rollers is produced by cadence alone. Competitors generally find two positions work: upright on the saddle, or down in the drops with legs unweighted. Warm-up techniques vary, but beer is popular as it relaxes the muscles. An aptitude for roller racing does not necessarily translate into cycling ability – some of the most unlikely people are good roller racers – but a roller race is a technically and physically demanding event, which actually closely mimics national cycling team talent tests. 'When they're testing out potential sprint athletes – on the Talent ID programme within the British Team – they do an unloaded cadence test,' explains Craig. 'Essentially, it's like doing a cadence test on your bike, fixed, with no resistance. I think that achieving around 250rpm, unloaded, indicates that someone is going to be a good sprinter.'

In corners of London, and on municipal basketball courts, in car parks and enclosed play areas around the world, bike polo has created a home.

Bicycle polo's first London home was the White City stadium, where men in bow ties mounted bicycles and contested an exhibition game at the 1908 Olympics. This version – on grass rather than concrete – was invented in Ireland by R. J. Mecredy, the editor of *Irish Cyclist* magazine, as he contemplated what to do when his racing career came to an end. On 4 October, 1891, he led 40 of the Ohne Haste CC to play 'polo on wheels' at the Scalp, County Wicklow. It was a hit, spreading like wildfire among the upper classes. It was quickly exported to India and the US, where cycling clubs and wheelmen around Long Island and upstate New York took to it enthusiastically.

'The scene is a novel one when the game is in full swing and players are moving swiftly here and there and making all manner of manoeuvres. Collisions are made but rarely,' reported the *New York Times* in 1895; the subject, a certain Francis Wilson and his daughters who 'ride their wheels like centaurs'. Wilson – erroneously – claimed to have invented the sport on his New Rochelle lawn.

In the Olympic match, Ireland beat Germany 3-1, and cycling clubs around the country took up the sport. After the Second World War, the Norwood Paragon was the dominant club in the UK, and London League teams played at the capital's

biggest football stadia, including Selhurst Park and Stamford Bridge. They rode highly specialized bikes, made by Claud Butler, Ching Allin and some of Britain's foremost builders of lightweight machines. A grass-pitch polo bicycle has a very short wheelbase, the better for manoeuvrability and hitting shots behind the back wheel; near 1:1 gearing, fixed; a pitched-back saddle, for control; riser bars and a short stem; and cranks as short as 145mm, again for ease of shooting under the bike. Wheels had up to 48 thick spokes, for durability, as they were often hit with mallets or used to block opponents' shots. Despite the Duke of Edinburgh being inspired to play at an exhibition match in 1967, grass-pitch polo declined as a generation of riders retired and was not replaced by fresh legs; its popularity worldwide is, however, now on the rise.

Right: An Allin grass polo bike photographed in the 1950s.
Below: Crystal Palace defend an attack by the Norwood Paragon, London 1948.

The hardcourt variant has its roots in Seattle's messenger community around 2003. Gradually, a loose bundle of rules evolved. Pitches are completely enclosed, usually the size of a tennis or basketball court; the goals, two traffic cones a bike's-width apart, are placed about 1.8m (6ft) from either end, so that play can carry on behind each. To score, the ball must be hit with the end of the mallet – usually fashioned out of a section of thick water pipe and a cut-down ski pole – forwards through the goal. At the beginning of a game, the ball is placed in the centre and, at the shout of '1, 2, 3, POLO!' two teams of three compete to be the first to score five.

Hardcourt is played worldwide. In Europe, players mainly ride fixed; in the US, anything goes – fixed, single-speed, MTB, mongrel, whatever. Just get a beater bike – or get ready to trash a new one – set it up on about a 50" gear, max, put on some shortish risers, or town bars at a pinch, and fashion a ghetto disc out of an estate agent's sign to protect the front wheel from bashes. Fixed allows more precise handling, easier speed modulation and the ability to reverse and to defend the goal by rocking back and forth. With good bike control, it is rare to see a player on fixed put his or her foot down, unless hit by another rider. If a foot goes down, that player must not touch the ball

Opposite: Polo bike courtesy of Mike and Roxy.
Above: European Hardcourt Bike Polo Showdown, Zurich 2008.
Right: Polo player, Milan.
Below right: The Pit, New York City.

again until they have tapped in – touched their mallet at a
fixed point at the court's edge, sometimes a bell. Running
a freewheel perhaps gives more stability and co-ordination
when trying to shoot at speed, thanks to the ability to coast.

Hardcourt polo is fast, skilful and slightly dangerous, a game
that reels people in and gets them addicted. Essentially all
it needs is a few friends, a few bikes, a few beers and an
expanse of concrete. It's a social occasion, good to watch
while waiting for a turn on court, sometimes tight and
technical, sometimes fluid and flowing, and crashes, scrapes
and spills are common. When there aren't league games
being played – the first hardcourt bike polo league took place
in London in 2008/9 – the ambience is relaxed. Throw-in
games, in which everyone chucks a mallet in and teams get
picked at random, add a fun, unpredictable element, and help
players of all abilities to improve. Proper team play, however,
is essential for advanced teamwork to evolve. An increasing
number of international tournaments are bringing players
together, with a collision of styles, speeds and levels of
aggression. With the inception of a World Federation, it looks
likely that the global community will become tighter, rules
standardized and skill levels will rise yet further.

Fixed riding is no longer only about sporting performance, or the preserve of a small group of dedicated riders on the street. Although still untainted by the worst aspects of commercialism, it has become a wider phenomenon in urban culture, boutiques and galleries.

The passion of a few has helped fixed riding filter slowly towards the cycling mainstream, and shops have sprung up worldwide to service the demand. 'When we first started selling Phil Wood hubs,' says Travis T of Freewheel San Francisco, 'Phil Wood was like, "What the hell?!" In the whole of the United States they'd sell maybe a pair a month to some racer in Wisconsin. We really had to twist their arm to do colours. The first batch of colours they did was pink, and that was because some cute girl rang them up and said, "I really want pink hubs." They were like, "Yuh, OK." Then they called me and I was like yeah, I'll take some pink hubs.'

An industry has built up around the bikes and their followers; and, like anything rising from the underground, it provokes bittersweet feelings – whether from messengers sick of the media attention they receive, or others involved in the culture, who have helped push it to prominence yet are nostalgic for the time when the beauty of track bikes still seemed a secret shared by a closed circle of initiates.

Previous page: Detail of Futura's collaboration with Colnago, initiated by La Carrera bike shop, Toronto.

This page: Keirin Culture Café, Berlin and their Look Ma No Brakes exhibition of Colnagos customized by Futura and Stash.

Opposite above: Freewheel, San Francisco; King Kog; and Trackstar, New York City.

Opposite below: Fully customizable 1:9 scale model track bikes by Pedal ID, Japan.

'I had a customer come in and ask me if I'd teach him how to stop. That totally freaked me out.'
Gina Marie, King Kog

Gina Marie runs the King Kog track bike boutique in Brooklyn: 'I remember when you'd see people riding by on these bikes, and be like, "I must know them," and you definitely did know them. Now I don't know any of them... We opened the store for our friends – to have a cool place to hang out, to make and sell stuff, a place to get parts.'

The art and the commerce around the fixed have grown because, simply put, people love the feeling of riding them, love old bikes, and love steel in particular. The aesthetics of the design, the craft and the feel of the ride all combine to produce something unique. 'When you look at it, it's such a simple machine, you can't help but see beauty in its simplicity. And riding it, too, to this day, it feels really pure and it's fun because it's a challenge, and you feel so connected to the bike,' says Travis T. 'But it's hard because it's become such a trendy culture. When there's Stüssy T-shirts of people riding fixed gears... you don't want it to sell out too much because you don't want it to be a trend that just dies eventually, you want it to be a trend that sticks and stays.'

Left column: Tour de Ville, London.
Above: 14 Bike Co shop, London.
Below: Brick Lane Bikes, London.

'Steel is real.' Old Skool Track

'You can use carbon, but carbon's got no soul,' says Graeme Obree. 'If it's about soul, then it's a steel bike. It hasn't got soul unless someone's filed a tube to shape and put it into a lug and silver-soldered it. A steel bike that's built by a framebuilder is a product of a craftsman. It's a matter of craft. Almost everything in our society is pressed or factory produced – mass-made, plasticized, aero-ized objects. Carbon bikes are part of that genre, whereas a hand-built steel frame isn't. It stands out in its beauty.'

There has been a long line of artists and designers from outside the cycling world who have recognized this beauty and have incorporated the bicycle in their work, or displayed them in galleries. And, in 2007, the Design Museum in London asked Ben Wilson, an industrial designer, to curate an exhibition for them, paying testament to the fixed gear.

Many in the cycling world have reciprocated the engagement, not least Antonio Colombo. He has run Columbus, his family's steel tubing business since 1977 and now also oversees Cinelli. Based near Milan, the company had a history in elegant furniture design before becoming legendary for manufacturing the tubing used by Italian bicycle builders from Pinarello to Masi to Colnago. 'The bicycle itself is modern art, and I've looked for the crossovers between art and bikes ever since I was young,' he says. 'Many of the avant-garde's works started with Duchamp's wheel. So being an art lover since I was a kid I always looked for works related to the bicycle. Since the nineteenth century the bicycle has maybe been the most reproduced man-made object by artists. You name an artist, he has made a bicycle, from Hopper to Lichtenstein to Warhol. I started to work with artists, asking them to design bicycles and other things in 1978/79.'

The following pages show some of the exhibitions, collaborations and design projects that have taken the fixed-gear bike beyond riding.

Above: Graf legend Futura with one of his custom Colnagos.
Below: Keith Haring's collaboration with Antonio Colombo.

'The Laser happened in a lucky period when I had many people collaborating with me, and not many big companies were around – like Trek, Specialized, and so on. In a sense it was the last steel masterpiece because it came just a moment before carbon came into the picture. It was a single project in a lucky period, without much competition.

'I am also an art collector, so during the 1980s, I remember, there was a design revolution in Italy and the US. The fashion system grew, it was a decade of silliness, happiness, there was a lot of excitement in life. Besides that, in the '80s I was in my thirties, so I was very socially active. I happened to buy a few pieces of art from Keith Haring, I had the opportunity to know him. He was working with Fiorucci, one of the originators of the fashion revolution. The whole Fiorucci shop in Milan, 1000 square metres, was painted by Keith, then there were parties for a week. I gave him a mountain bike, a Multifluo, five colours, fluorescent, all mixed together, disco style. He loved it, it was an icon of a certain way of living in the '80s. He was excited to have a bicycle from me, and he was willing to give me a painting in exchange. I said, "Don't give me a piece of art; do a bicycle for me."

'I sent him a Laser bicycle and he sent it back two years later, painted. He came to Milan, we went to have lunch. We were friends, in a way. At that time he was quite accessible. He came to be a star, but while he was living he wasn't unreachable, he was a person you could work with. He was more known in Europe than New York. He'd work on anything it was possible to paint on. It was an obsession, to paint on everything.'

ANTONIO COLOMBO

'For the 25th anniversary of the Air Force One trainer, Acyde from Nike chose six different designers and artists to create something to celebrate. He wanted something hand-crafted because an Italian master shoemaker was making 100 pairs of AF1s, white on white - using artisan techniques to recreate a production shoe, a kind of reverse.

'Originally AF1s were worn by basketball players, who played matches throughout New York's five boroughs. They hung out with hip-hop artists, b-boys and graffiti writers, so the trainers became legendary because of the social circles they were mixing in.

'Nike didn't tell us to make a fixed-gear bike: I was considering building a bike, and Oscar and I thought the analogy with cycle messengers was apt. They're interesting people who move through different areas quickly, delivering maybe an important legal document, dropping off a prototype, or carrying medical samples across town. In society they mix with lots of different people, and they also have a certain unique style.

'I'd built many frames before, but very unconventionally. England has a long tradition of hand-built lugged frames, and that was important for me. The lugs are in stainless steel so

the accents are in silver - signifying the 25 years. On our blog we show in depth every stage of the fabrication process, it's very open source. The process is as important as the finished thing.

'I'd been travelling a lot and fixed gears were really bubbling on the streets of Tokyo, New York and other world cities. Now you can get components anodized in any colour, but in 2006 the parts weren't available. You couldn't buy Deep Vs in Britain and we stove-enamelled the hubs - but had to be careful of bearing tolerances. I wanted to mix a lot of styles but build something exclusive, kind of my dream bike. I grew up riding BMX and most of my bikes are single-speed, because that's what I know. For me, there's no wrong or right way to build a bike, but simplicity is the key.

'We don't ride the bike, it's sort of absurd: it's boxfresh, like collectors keep trainers. I like the fact it will always remain the same, depicting a past era through its style. For me and my brother, it conjured up what we saw on the streets at that time. Since then things have moved so quickly, there are so many amazing people building frames around the world.'

BEN WILSON

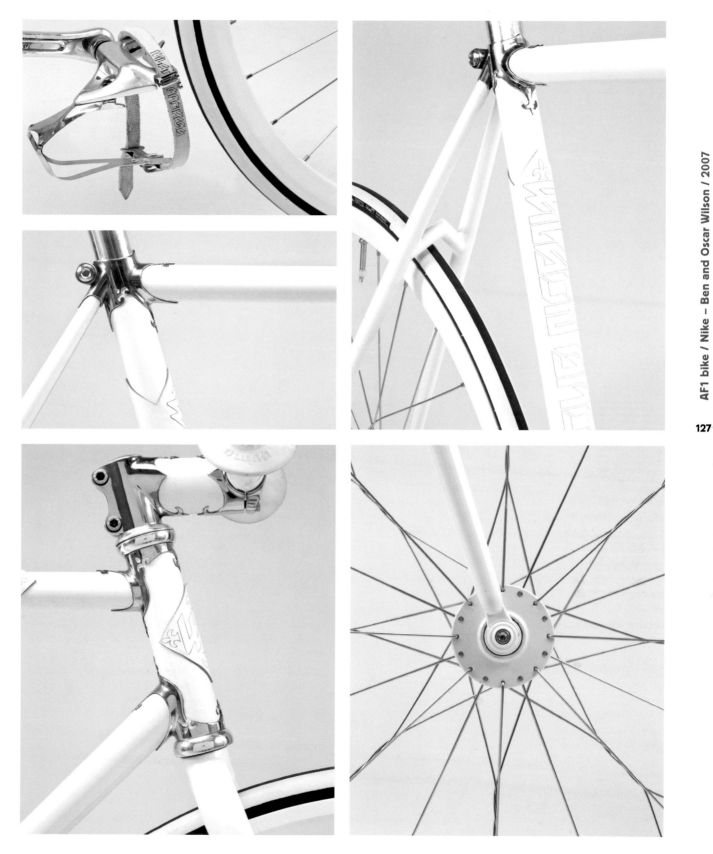

'I used to have a fixed-wheel, an old Claud Butler, which I rode to work every day. When I started track riding as a schoolboy, I rode a Paramount. Actually, it was made by Mercian from Derby, but the little shop just outside of Nottingham was called Paramount.

'I used to have my bike in my bedroom; I loved it as an object so much I used to take it to bed with me! Especially when I had my first bike, the Mercian/Paramount, built. It was so beautiful to look at. I suppose there was a designer in me then. It was yellow, with Campag everything, and I used it for pursuits. I'm not built for sprinting, so I went pursuiting. The great thing about pursuiting is that you can only come second or first! Then, at the age of seventeen, I crashed while training, broke a femur and ended up in hospital for a long time. How I describe it is that I literally fell into fashion.

'Mercian were turning sixty, and knew I'd had one, so they asked to put a bike in one of my shops. I said, "Why don't we collaborate?" I didn't design the bike, I just customized it really, because the bike is beautiful in its own right... Isn't it nice to think that something is still made in Britain with such passion and by hand? The only thing I wanted to do was have the old transfer on the front, and use a Brooks saddle with the big rivets.

'The flip-flop colour idea is a visual joke. I used to do a shirt where the front was one colour and the back was another, I called it the "coming and going shirt". You could arrive in a restaurant, eat your meal and run out without paying and people would say: "The guy that was here was in a red shirt, but I didn't see anybody in a red shirt leave!" You can lean the bike against a shop, and it's yellow, but ride it away and it'll be red.

'My Mercian, which they made to measure, is matt black. It's a lovely thing, a made-to-measure bike.'

PAUL SMITH

'These frames are based on the M1 production art series, when BMW asked famous artists to paint the cars, then took them to be raced on the track – million-dollar cars with million-dollar paint jobs bumping against each other. That's the way I always saw these Colnago Masters – they're true racing bikes.

'Ernesto Colnago to me is the Enzo Ferrari of bicycles. I wanted his view of the winningest bike in history. The frame's made with special tubing that he picked, it had to be re-issued by Columbus, and Colnago had to re-tool the factory for these frames. The Stash are hand-painted, the Futura are hand-laid stickers, the dots colour-matched based on swatches on his computer. The company that did the art is based in Pisa. They did the Colnago Forever bike and also restore major cathedrals in Italy. They hated the Futura bike! They had to hand-lay every single dot.

'The total production of these bikes was 76: 38 of Stash, 38 of Futura, we thought it was a cool number. There are 12 prototypes, and two road prototypes that I own. There were 12 additional frames in 60 and 62cm that were built, but they're being destroyed. My commitment to the buyers and the artists was that only 76 would be produced. It has to be done, even though it's hurtful to me. The frames are being stripped, they're being painted in the Molteni colours and they're going to be sent back to me.

'I just built up the last Futura bike we did, the only one we did in 60cm, for a professor of mathematics at the University of Toronto. He wants to build it to ride it, to piss people off, I think that's really cool. Actually, a few people have chased down Futura just so they can see the bike, and they don't realize it's actually him riding it. In New York his is the only one.

'Stash and Futura both have one, which they ride. Stash is the most natural person I've seen on a track bike right off the bat. He was skidding straight off. He let one rip in a second!'

NADIR OLIVET, OWNER, LA CARRERA BIKE SHOP, TORONTO

'When Nadir invited me to join the project, I was a bit intimidated, but I always enjoy a design challenge. It was a PIMP MY RIDE situation. As there is not a lot of workable surface, I tried to convey PURE CADENCE using arrows, and I typically use the colour blue so also incorporated my colour palette.

'The first fixed gear I rode was the Colnago I designed – one spin and I picked it right up and i've been riding ever since. I like to say "TRACK BIKES ARE THE NEW CRACK."'

STASH, ARTIST

'I've been into bikes for a long time, I was really into BMX as a kid. It's always made sense to me to ride bikes. My friend Erik Zo let me try his Cinelli fixed gear in front of my studio some 15 years ago. It was completely exhilarating racing around the neighbourhood at 2am.

'The fascination with rusty steel frames came a few months later. I love things that rust. I'm super into anything steel, that goes for old cars and all that stuff. A good friend, and tagging partner Josh Lazcano brought me a late fifties Bob Matthews which was covered in flaky rust and grey paint. A few weeks later he found me an old Bob Jackson track, red with white pinstripes and incredible lug work. These two steel-framed relics were the inspiration for the Cinelli bike project.

'The Cinelli project was a fantastic project. I started out with all these other things, like patterns on it, it was fluorescent, but I felt it was too trendy, I wanted it to fit the partner, and Cinelli are just classic. I wanted it to be looser and with brighter colours, but when it came down to it, I just wanted it to be a classic bike. They're classic colours, which I'm glad about. There are a lot of really bright coloured track bikes around the city right now, so it already seems old. It seems like something out of the '60s, early '70s or something. Everything was in place, everything was good then.

'I would have just been happy doing a head badge, you know. I mean it's Cinelli, I think Antonio runs his whole company as an art project. Just to be able to draw anything on there, I was ecstatic. They wanted to use more modern Cinelli logos and I asked if we could use the old ones, and they were like yeah, sure. I was really happy about that too.It's a nod to the past.'

BARRY MCGEE, ARTIST

Andy Ellis tests the prototype FGL/Vans bike.

'Vans released the "Fixed" shoes and we were going to do a bike with the colours and all that. But we wanted to do everything as seriously as possible, so instead of getting any old bike and painting it, we had the idea to try and build a bike. We'd seen loads of collaboration bikes and all the companies do is get a bike and slap their logo on. Vans could have done that, but we pushed them to do something completely different. It's our idea of what it would look like if Vans were to make a bike.'

ANDY ELLIS

'The idea was to build a bike to go along with the shoe. I'd done a framebuilding course with Dave Yates and had been thinking about building frames a lot. Then this opportunity came up, so I thought, if we're going to build a bike, I'm gonna build a frame for it... I had to build a jig for it and everything, though. We wanted to make something kind of in a BMX style, like a Vans bike should look, but not like a tricks-specific bike that is really burly. It's really strong, because of the fillet brazing, but it looks clean and not overweight. It's got oval tubing and a really slim rear end. The paint job really makes it; it's got the Vans style – the checkerboard texture and relief.'

SUPERTED

'We know certain things about riding track bikes on the street – what works, and what works better. We took that information and designed a track bike frame with Cinelli.

'Cinelli has always been a company that, in terms of riding a track bike on the street, has a pretty rich history. Cinelli have their heart in the right place, so we waited for the right person and decided to go from there.'

GARRETT CHOW

'In 2005 Trackstar made a Mash spoof video, *NashNYC*. We were floored, like, "Damn, that's the highest form of flattery!" Trackstar had ripped off the Columbus bird for one of their logos, so as a throwback, we made a Mashstar T with the Columbus logo dead bird. Third-generation copyright infringement! I met Luigi from Cinelli at the first Hand Made Bike Show in San Jose, gave him some Ts and a copy of a Mash short. Later, Antonio hit me up and was grossed out, and proud of this circle of logo thieves on classic bikes.

'We'd had several offers to develop with other brands, but wanted to produce with someone small enough that we would not get lost in a brand, and someone that had rich race history. Our hearts were always with Cinelli. As Europe began to get into the bikes in 2006, then in Italy seeing it grow more in '07, Cinelli became more interested and we were ready to move forward.

'The design process was inspiring. To work closely with their team, with all their experience, to produce a frame we had not experienced yet – Cinelli had never produced a duel-700c mild pursuit frame. Our goal was to design a frame we would want to ride. We wanted an aluminium frame and carbon fork, with a more aggressive geometry, that let your body get into a more upright position for day-to-day traffic and get low and fast for logging miles. We hope riders find this balance inspiring, fast, stiff and, no, it does not barspin.'

MIKE MARTIN

'I was a total stranger to fixed-gear culture, but was overwhelmed by the beauty, quality and simplicity of Uula Jero's bike when he came to an opening once. For me it was a beautiful object; a sculpture on wheels.

'What fascinates me in art is the spirit, enthusiasm, commitment and the soul of the artist, which you can sense in the artist's work. Uula manages to combine (well-researched and homaged) history with design. Naturally, environmental issues and recycled materials are in the spotlight too. He even manages to add scent to his bikes by using tarred cord.

'By simplifying and stripping down he adds a personal touch, leaving room for the essential: a functional beauty. Uula's bikes enable a physical artistic experience.'

TIINA AALTONEN
GALLERY GRAPPO, HELSINKI, FINLAND

'Since the time motors replaced mechanical innovations, our Western world has been racing to improve the quality of living on this planet through wasteful means. This pursuit seems to deny all boundaries.

The bicycle is the most efficient means of transportation known to man. Modern society evolves, technological advances morph cycling as we know it, the truth fades. This simple and functional device is falling into the category of the esoteric. One could call this path misleading, since the true form of the bicycle lies beneath the fancy derailleur and powerful disc-brake systems.

Functionally disentangled, the bicycle is a natural extension of human capability. It becomes a tool in its true meaning. As natural as walking, it provides a response to every muscular procedure and under trained control its agility has no match.

In my interpretation, concentrating on essential function and semantics, I used salvaged bicycles and parts, giving them a new form and use through simplification. The work guided me to discover the beauty of this misunderstood machine.'

UULA JERO, ARTIST

'As much as fixed-gear riding is about pure joy, it is also a rebellion against cookie-cutter life. It is about bending the rules, disobeying traffic laws, wearing no helmet, using no brakes in the streets.

'The simplicity of the bike and its mechanism make it the ideal white canvas for expressing creativity. The exhibition showcases fixed-gear bikes and their riders in Los Angeles and Berlin, two cities connected by that same creative spirit.'

EXHIBITION CATALOGUE TEXT

Acknowledgements

We would like to thank:

Brooklands Museum and Bob French, Jos and Keith - Tour de Ville, SuperTed and Andy - Fixed Gear London, Max - Tokyo Fixed Gear, Roxy and Mike, Ian Sansom and Nick Butterfield - Fixed Mag, Buffalo Bill, Winston and Caspar - Rollapaluza, David Higman, Peter Wall, Eddie Wingrave, Velocio and www.londonfgss.com, Gabes, Plagiarist, Flickwg, Chris Lovibond, Matt Seaton.

Chris Boardman, Graeme Obree, Craig MacLean, Lee Povey, Terry Dolan, Grant, Jane and all at Mercian, Katy - Face Partnership, Richard Truman and Abby Burton - British Cycling.

Squid and Amy Bolger, Nelson Vails, Fast Eddie Williams, Gina and Fleming - King Kog, Joe, Luke and Seth - Brooklyn Machine Works, Brooklyn Jack Crank, Mark 'that's original' McLean, everyone at Trackstar, Amy Burns, Jake Steadman, Pedro and Miguel, Vince Moore and Doug - Old Skool Track, Gerry Lopez, Victor Blast, Jason and Craig - Affinity, Larry Dufus, Fisher from Condor (via Larry and Jeff's), Katz's Deli.

Antonio, Fabrizio, Alessandra and Paolo - Gruppo, Pasquale and Fabio Bellotti - Bianchi, Alessandro and Ernesto Colnago, Eric Von Munz - Cog.

Mike, Gabe and Garrett - Mash SF, Colin, Colby, Jason, Rainier, Steve and Phil - Macaframa, Travis T and Dustin - Freewheel, Dennis Peron, Chad, Tim Brooks.

Ben and Oscar Wilson, Barry McGee, Nadir Olivet - La Carrera, Futura, Stash, John Benson - Project Dragon, Remi / Rough, Paul Smith, Colette Youell.

Pai, Eisuke, Sino, Hal, Akira and John   Kinfolk, Tomity, Yohei and all at W-Base, Eli Chessen, Hisashi and Buchi - Paul Smith Japan, Kory Biggs, Ichi - BFF Tokyo, Koichi Nakano, Tatsu, Enamoto, Goseki and everyone at JKA, Sato, Murakami and the guys at Keirin School, Tanabe-san - Kalavinka.

Maria Laub, Mortimer - Keirin Berlin, Ed Scoble, Jocelyn Low, Tom Oldham, Cédric Viollet, Kyle Johnson, Greg Falski, Lorne Shields, Helen Ford and the staff of the Modern Records Centre, Warwick.

Bycaboy, Lewis from Lewes, Elvis, Guerillaphoto, Kelvin, Kaiser Minelli and Filmore Scolari.

Ryo and Shaz - SRK.

Kevin Mason, Matthew Halls, Adam Bronkhorst - Garage Studios, Jo Lightfoot, Sophie Page and everyone at Laurence King.

Last but not least, thanks to Jan Heine, editor of *Bicycle Quarterly*, for a chat about *porteurs*, and to Les Woodland, whose *Unknown Tour de France* (Van der Plas Publications/Cycle Publishing San Francisco) was an invaluable source for early racing facts, and is well worth buying. Likewise, Peter Joffre Nye's *The Six Day Bicycle Races, America's Jazz-Age Sport* (also Van der Plas publications) was equally helpful and fascinating. Finally, Michael Hutchinson's book, *The Hour* (Yellow Jersey Press), is amazing and funny. It's to him that we owe the wonderful Eddy Merckx quote.

And anyone we forgot along the way.

Sheldon Brown, RIP

Picture credits

Photographer / archive source	Page reference
Johannes Aaltonen	138 (top: hub and lug detail)
Adward	100, 118
Colin Arlen and Colby Elrick	78, 81, 82, 83 (top), 98
© Diego Azubel / epa / Corbis	20
Amy Bolger	64, 70, 74 (top two rows), 76 (bottom)
Lucas Brunelle	108-9
© David Cannon / Getty Images	60
Cinelli and Gruppo Spa	123 (bottom), 124, 125, 132, 133, 136, 137
darkdaze.org	14, 15 (bottom and top rows), 39
Andrew Edwards	15 (middle), 35 (top right), 43, 50-53, 55, 58, 59, 62 (left), 67, 83 (bottom right), 84 (except middle row, right two), 88, 90, 91 (bottom), 92 (left two), 93, 101, 117 (bottom), 121, 122 (middle and bottom left)
Roxy Erickson	107 (top), 114, 117 (top)
Fhai	77 (top)
Angelo Giangregorio	77 (bottom left), 117 (middle)
gregfalski.com	99 (bottom), 102 (bottom)
M. Halls / Garage Studios	5, 7, 11, 13, 22-29, 32 (top), 33 (bottom), 56, 57, 116, 126, 127, 134, 135, 142
Bert Hardy, Hulton Archive / Getty Images	115 (bottom)
Mike Hewitt / Getty Images	21
Courtesy of David Higman and the National Cycle Collection	8, 111 (top right)
Courtesy of Hounslow and District Wheelers	31
Kai Ilchmann	106, 122 (top row, middle and bottom right)
JKA	44-49, 54 (bottom)
Uula Jero	138 (except top two), 139
Kyle Johnson	74 (bottom right), 77 (bottom right), 103
Walter Lai	119, 130, 131
Library of Congress	72, 110
Maria Laub	54 (top), 68, 69, 75, 76 (top), 120, 123 (top)
Max Leonard	94 (top)
Jocelyn Low	112 (top), 113 (top right)
Mike Martin and Gabe Morford	79, 83 (bottom, except far right), 84 (middle row, right two), 85, 86, 87, 137
© Leonard McCombe / Getty Images	61
National Cycle Archive	9 (top), 32 (bottom)
Courtesy of Graeme Obree	33 (right), 41
Offside / L'Equipe	10, 12, 36, 37, 38, 73
Franz Otto, courtesy of Visual Research, Berlin	140 (right column)
Pai	74 (bottom left), 91 (top), 92 (right two)
© Gary M. Prior / Getty Images	40
Rollapaluza / Tom Oldham	112, 113 (middle left, and bottom row)
SSPL / Science Museum	9 (bottom)
Edward Scoble	107 (bottom)
From the collection of Lorne Shields, Canada	18
Courtesy of Paul Smith	128, 129
Bernard Thompson	30, 33 (left), 34, 35 (top left)
© Underwood & Underwood / Corbis	16, 17
Cédric Viollet	102 (top), 104-5
Courtesy of Visual Research, Berlin	140 (left column), 141
Peter Wall	115 (top)
Bryan Ward	19
Eddie Williams	63, 65, 66, 112 (bottom)
Eddie Wingrave	111 (except top right)
Paul Wright	35 (bottom)
X-ray Sexysushi	89, 94 (bottom), 95, 96, 99 (top)
Avalo York	62 (right)

We have done everything we can to gain permission to use these images. If you think you own the copyright to an image we have used, please contact us.